BROTHERS OF UJIMA

A Cultural Enrichment Program to Empower Adolescent African American Males

Faye Z. Belgrave | Kevin W. Allison | Jerome Wilson | Raymond Tademy

2612 North Mattis Avenue ◈ Champaign, Illinois 61822 ◈ (800) 519-2707 ◈ www.researchpress.com

5 4 3 2 1 12 13 14 15 16

Copies of this book may be ordered from Research Press
at the address given on the title page.

Composition by Jeff Helgesen
Cover design by Linda Brown, Positive I.D. Graphic Design, Inc.
Printed by Seaway Printing Co.

ISBN: 978-0-87822-652-8
Library of Congress Control Number 2011932198

Contents

Acknowledgments

Several individuals contributed to the development of this manual. The initial prototype was a female cultural curriculum called *Sisters of Nia* developed by a team headed by Dr. Valerie Cherry at Progressive Life Center, now in Tampa, Florida, along with Dr. Faye Belgrave at Virginia Commonwealth University.

Individuals within the Richmond Metro Area Boys and Girls Club and Sacred Heart Community Center worked with us in Richmond, Virginia. We thank all of the boys who enthusiastically participated in our program in Richmond and their parents who entrusted their sons to us. Also thanks to Dr. Maya Corneille and Vivian Lucas, who were instrumental in helping to evaluate and coordinate the program, and Deborah Butler, who provided administrative support.

The implementation of our curriculum was supported by grants from the Center for Substance Abuse Prevention. We are appreciative of Frances Johnson and Jeanne DiLoreto and other project officers who encouraged and supported our efforts.

Introduction

Many African American preadolescent and adolescent boys face challenges linked to residing in low-income and low-resource urban communities. Some risk factors include low academic achievement and life-course expectations, and involvement in delinquent activities. Although African American adolescent males are no more likely to use drugs than boys in other ethnic groups, they are more likely to be exposed to drugs and related problems in their community. Yet many of our boys show strengths, including high self-worth, positive relationships with adults, spiritual connectedness, positive relationships with peers, good sportsmanship, and other pro-social behaviors.

The *Brothers of Ujima* program is aimed at reinforcing and bringing out the strengths of these boys. *Ujima* is a Kiswahili word that means "collective work and responsibility." It represents the importance of boys working together to achieve goals for themselves, their families, and their communities. For example, most have high goals, but some don't know how to achieve them. They may not be able to connect their current behaviors or the behaviors of those around them with their future goals. *Brothers of Ujima* seeks to bridge this divide. Studies have shown that culturally relevant intervention programs can give these boys some of the direction, relationship skills, identity empowerment, and critical consciousness that lead to more positive self-esteem and relationships with others, greater ethnic pride, and higher expectations for future accomplishments.

This curriculum is primarily for preadolescent and adolescent boys ages 10 to 14, who are in a stage when developmental changes coincide with other changes such as the transitions from elementary to middle school and middle to high school. During this stage, boys' goals, behaviors, and personalities are developing—not just their bodies. They are in the process of learning from their environment how to be men. Older boys ages 15 to 16 may also benefit from this curriculum.

The *Brothers of Ujima* program is a supplemental environment from which young African American men can learn. The program can serve as a rite of passage that complements other efforts within the family, school, or community. The program's objectives are as follows:

- To help students gain an understanding of the *Nguzo Nane* (Eight Principles for Living)
- To increase knowledge of and appreciation for African and African American culture
- To encourage pursuit of physical health and fitness
- To encourage critical awareness of myths and stereotypes of African Americans presented in the media
- To develop creative thinking and leadership skills
- To strengthen personal goal setting and commitment to education
- To develop positive ways of coping and handling conflict
- To increase knowledge of local community history
- To increase awareness of adult role models within the African American community

To accomplish these objectives, the program helps participants do the following:

- Learn about and from successful African American male role models
- Learn about and participate in African cultural activities and traditions
- Become aware of stereotypes and racism and how to deal with them in community and media messages
- Become aware of negative behaviors and their consequences
- Engage in team-building activities and discussions designed to promote positive relationships with other males
- Learn the Eight Principles for African American Living (*Nguzo Nane*) and discover how they can be applied to one's

functioning in everyday life in the home, school, and community

Programs for African American boys must consider the unique aspects of their culture and their environment. Mentoring and cultural socialization can have many positive effects on behaviors and life outcomes. We believe that this program will not only be valued by the boys who participate in it but by those who carry them out. In implementing the program and helping to create "Brothers of Ujima," you will become one yourself.

FACILITATOR'S GUIDE

CURRICULUM OVERVIEW

The *Brothers of Ujima* curriculum is a 14-week cultural enrichment curriculum for African American preadolescent and adolescent boys, ages 10 to 14. The curriculum is designed to foster positive behaviors and to reduce negative behaviors among boys in this age range. Participants are organized into *jamaas*, or small groups, of no more than eight boys each. *Jamaa* means family in Kiswahili, and the small group format is meant to symbolize a family unit, at least while the boys are in session. An *mzee*, or respected elder, in this case young adult male, facilitates each *jamaa*. Each *mzee* is responsible for working as a member of the program's facilitating team, as well as for leading each two-hour session of his *jamaa*.

The Seven Principles of Kwanzaa (*Nguzo Saba*), plus an eighth principle—the principle of *Heshema*, or respect—provide the framework for the sessions. These seven principles, developed by Maulana Karenga in 1966 as a celebration of African American heritage, coupled with African proverbs, serve as guiding themes for the sessions. Through discussion, guest speakers, activity demonstrations, journaling, and application of the lessons outside of the program space, the boys explore and integrate these principles into their own lives and so move toward their goals. In keeping with the Africentric focus, the program integrates a number of words from the Kiswahili language. These words are defined as they appear; in addition, a glossary, including phonetic pronunciations, appears at the back of this book.

Africentric Methods

In traditional African families and historically in African American families, raising children and helping them move toward adulthood were the responsibility of the community. This philosophy undergirds *Brothers of Ujima*, which targets boys growing up here in the United States, where connections to community do not always exist. The program uses methods and strategies that focus on both community and individual responsibility. These elements include *mzees*, *jamaas*, the *durara umoja*, *tambiko*, the call and response, the *Nguzo Nane*, and sessions about African history and culture.

The program's *mzees*, or leaders, are modeled on their traditional counterparts. *Mzees* not only act as facilitators for each session, they also serve as accessible mentors and role models for the boys, just as they do in traditional African culture. Each *mzee* works with a group of boys called a *jamaa*, or family. Each *jamaa* selects a name that symbolizes an African value, character, or tribe and, in that naming, becomes a small family of individuals responsible for one another's well-being.

The *durara umoja* (unity circle) and *tambiko* (libations) are key rituals performed in each session. The *mzees* and participants (as well as any guest speakers who are present) form the *durara umoja* at the beginning and end of each session. This reminds the boys that they are not only members of their *jamaa* but also members of the larger *Brothers of Ujima* community and the larger community outside of the program. Libations, or *tambiko*, are poured in honor of the ancestors at the beginning of each session. In the *Brothers of Ujima* program, *tambiko* usually takes the form of water poured on the soil of a plant to symbolize the renewal of life that comes with honoring the ancestors. It is believed that so long as we speak the names of our ancestors, they will never be lost to us.

Mzees use the call and response method to gather the *jamaas* together for the *durara umoja* or at any other time everyone's attention is needed. In the call and response, an *mzee* calls out an agreed-upon word or phrase, to which the entire group calls out an agreed-upon response. (Military cadences are somewhat similar.) In our groups, we have used the term *agoo*, and the boys reply, *amee*. *Agoo* means, roughly, "Attention," and *amee* is the acknowledgment, "I'm listening." These words are from the Twi language of the Akan people of Ghana, West Africa.

Each session is built on one or more of the following Eight Principles for African American Living (*Nguzo Nane*):

1. *Umoja:* Unity
2. *Kujichagulia:* Self-Determination
3. *Ujima:* Collective Work and Responsibility (Teamwork)
4. *Ujamaa:* Cooperative Economics
5. *Nia:* Purpose
6. *Kuumba:* Creativity

7. *Imani:* Faith
8. *Heshema:* Respect

Two of the 14 sessions are dedicated to African history and culture. In these sessions, the boys face their own misconceptions and misinformation about Africa. This erroneous knowledge is then replaced with reliable information about African history and culture, with a special emphasis on some of Africa's historical kings and leaders and on Africans' great contributions to the world.

Session Topics

Session 1: Orientation

This session introduces boys to the program, allows *mzees* and participants to get to know one another, and introduces boys to the methods and vocabulary of the program.

Session 2: Jamaa Building

In this session, the *jamaas* or family groups are formed. The purpose of the *jamaas* is explained and boys name their *jamaa*. Boys set up the rules for their *jamaas* and they begin to understand the methods of the program.

Nguzo/Principle: Nia (Purpose)

Session 3: Health and Fitness

This session helps the boys to understand the role of nutrition, rest, and exercise in being healthy and physically fit. The session also helps boys to begin to understand ways of supporting each other.

Nguzo/Principle: Kujichagulia (Self-Determination)

Session 4: My Brother's Keeper

This session enhances boys' understanding of how negative myths about African American males can have harmful effects. It also encourages the boys' feelings of responsibility to each other.

Nguzo/Principle: Umoja (Unity)

Session 5: Introduction to Africa and African American Culture—Fact and Fiction

Session 6: African and African American Culture—Yesterday and Today

These two sessions increase knowledge and appreciation of Africa and its culture, correct stereotypes of Africa and African people, and help boys see their connection to Africa.

Nguzo/Principle: Umoja (Unity)

Session 7: What Do I Bring to My Community?

This session helps the boys to think more about their community and what they can do to benefit their community.

Nguzo/Principle: Ujamaa (Cooperative Economics)

Session 8: Creativity

This session introduces boys to forms of creative expression and provides an opportunity for them to express their own creativity.

Nguzo/Principle: Kuumba (Creativity)

Session 9: Educational Awareness

This session increases awareness of the importance of education and cultivation of knowledge and helps the boys to think about how education can expand their opportunities.

Nguzo/Principle: Nia (Purpose)

Session 10: Life Course

This session encourages the boys to think about their future and how they can use their talents and gifts to achieve their goals.

Nguzo/Principle: Imani (Faith)

Session 11: Choices and Challenges

This session supports the boys in examining strategies for successfully handling difficult and challenging situations they may face in everyday life.

Nguzo/Principle: Kujichagulia (Self-Determination)

Session 12: How Do I Work It Out?

This session discusses positive ways in which conflict can be resolved.

Nguzo/Principle: Heshema (Respect)

Session 13: African American Male Leadership

This session increases boys' knowledge of how to be leaders within their families and community. The session also familiarizes the boys with positive African American male leaders.

Nguzo/Principle: Ujima (Collective Work and Responsibility)

Session 14: Graduation and Closing Ceremony

This final session helps each boy to understand his inner self and the positive ways in which he is viewed by others. The graduation is also held at this session.

Optional Session: Kwanzaa

If it is the appropriate time of year, you can introduce participants to—or reinforce their knowledge of—the Kwanzaa celebration. This session offers boys the opportunity to learn the history and symbolism of the holiday, lets them know that the holiday does not replace Christmas or Hanukkah, builds *jamaa* unity, and allows the boys to express their creativity.

Suggested Field Trip(s)

If funds and time are available, plan an outing with your boys—hiking a trail, taking a nature walk, canoeing, or a similar activity. These activities build confidence, further develop unity, and may introduce the boys to a previously unknown talent, stress reducer, or interest. You may also consider local or regional trips centered around relevant cultural resources. Examples include performances of African drumming and dance; African or African American art and history museums or historical societies; local historical sites relevant to African American history; performances of African or African American plays, music, or poetry; Step Shows; or HBCUs in the area. Depending on your location, some groups may consider travel to the Smithsonian National Museum of African Art.

SETTING UP THE PROGRAM

This program can be run as an after-school program in schools, churches, or community centers, or it can be conducted in any other available space in which adult supervision and desire exist. It can be used as a stand-alone curriculum or in conjunction with other programs, such as those devoted to academic tutoring, conflict management, or substance abuse prevention. A group or program wishing to set up a *Brothers of Ujima* program will need to recruit participants, identify and train *mzees*, invite guest speakers, obtain the necessary materials for each session, and arrange for space to hold the meetings. The following discussion suggests some ways to accomplish these tasks.

Community Resources

Volunteers make the *Brothers of Ujima* program possible; therefore, people are your first priority. Local colleges and universities, civic and volunteer organizations, sororities, churches, sporting leagues, and community centers are good places to look for help. If you are seeking material donations, check with local business owners who might like to contribute funds or supplies. Other organizations focusing on youth development (e.g., Boys and Girls Clubs) or local foundations and community support organizations (e.g., United Way) may also be able to direct you to potential resources and partners. First and foremost, be creative, assertive, and diligent in your search for community resources. Be bold enough to ask whether people are willing to help.

Establishing a Community of Elders (Optional)

Building a more formal group of elders and supporting organizations can be very useful in the implementation of the program. Such a group strengthens the program's continuity and provides a means for linking youth participants to ongoing support and resources in the community. Well-known and trusted individuals and organizations that are knowledgeable about African and African American culture and adolescent development can be engaged to form an established group of elders supporting the *Brothers* program. Members of this group can work to connect youth to positive opportunities (e.g., tutoring, arts and athletic programs, mentoring, scholarships, employment). They can serve as presenters within relevant program sessions or as interview subjects (see activity option, Session 4). They can also attend and participate in opening and closing sessions, and they can raise funds. Established organizations like Big Brothers and Big Sisters can provide linkages to ongoing mentoring. Take great care to identify safe resources; if you are identifying individuals who will work directly with youth, require background checks (e.g., child abuse reports from social service agencies and criminal records through state police). Local and national cultural groups are often important resources in identifying community elders [See groups such as 100 Black Men, fraternities, the NAACP, the Urban League or the local Minority Business League, or explore collaboration with rites of passage programs (e.g., http://www.ritesofpassage.org/)].

Finding and Choosing *Mzees*

Mzees, or group leaders, are integral to the program. They facilitate the groups and act as models for participants. Therefore, finding and choosing appropriate *mzees* is one of the most important tasks in creating a successful *Brothers of Ujima* program. In order to have the most productive program possible, *mzees* must possess certain characteristics. Specifically, *mzees* should be African American or other males of African ancestry (Jamaican, Afro-Brazilian, Ghanaian, Egyptian, etc.), at least seven years older than the participants, with a minimum age of 19. An *mzee* in this age range provides a clear example of what the boys can achieve in the next stage of their maturity. If still in college, *mzees* should be good students and value education and academic development. This does not mean that these individuals must share the educational philosophy of all mainstream institutions, but that these individuals understand and value the individual, group, and cultural importance of knowledge development. It may also be valuable to choose as *mzees* students who have dramatically improved in school, as a mirroring technique. In such cases, the level of improvement may be more important than a high grade-point average.

Since a diverse group of boys of different stages of maturity will participate in the program and boys may bring a range of experience surrounding relationships with adults, *mzees* must be patient, sociable, and punctual. Consistency, including attendance, is key. It also helps if *mzees* share at least some of the same social or economic conditions as the participants. It goes without saying that leadership qualities are also essential. Most important, *mzees* must have demonstrated values similar to those articulated by the program. These values include interest in African and African American culture, positive value for education, and commitment to improving the lives of youth.

It is also desirable to find male *mzees* who have some interest in a range of physical, creative, and expressive activities, including athletics and sports or music and other creative arts. These are venues for connecting boys to *mzees*. The ability to effectively engage and support the development of boys with varied interests may depend on the *mzees'* ability to be inclusive but willing to meet boys where they are. However, meeting youth where they are does not mean simply staying there. In part, the program works by supporting boys in moving beyond narrow and stereotypical notions of African American manhood. *Mzees* should also have values of inclusiveness and should be committed to the positive development of African American male youth. They should be nonjudgmental and acknowledge diverse views on a range of individual and social issues (e.g., religion, sexual orientation, athletic ability, cultural values, health status). *Mzees* should be models of respect. Special care should be taken to ensure that *mzees* demonstrate respect to women and elders and do not engage in sexism, ageism, or other forms of disrespect.

Finally, prospective *mzees* must be able to meet the following time commitments:

- Four hours per week for the duration of the program (14 to 16 weeks, depending on the inclusion of optional Kwanzaa and field-trip activities). The four hours per week includes two and a half hours of program implementation, an hour-long staff meeting, and 30 minutes of session preparation.
- A one-time *mzee* training session. The duration of this session is at the discretion of the implementation team, but five hours is a minimum.

Sample *Mzee* Training Session

There are six main objectives of the *mzee* training session:

Objective 1: To build a cooperative foundation so that facilitators are able to work as a team

Objective 2: To educate *mzees* on development at the preadolescent and adolescent stages, with an emphasis on behavior and cognition

Objective 3: To educate *mzees* on issues relevant to African American boys

Objective 4: To familiarize and educate *mzees* on Africentric methods and reinforce Africentric values

Objective 5: To provide instruction in effective group facilitation and teaching strategies

Objective 6: To offer information about the structure and strategies of the curriculum

Let these six objectives serve as your agenda for the session. Objective 1 can be realized through discussion of your reasons for implementing or participating in the program, or by doing other team-building activities.

Short presentations by guest speakers and cultural specialists (including African American educators, psychologists, counselors, and cultural studies scholars) can help you realize Objectives 2, 3, and 4. In lieu of such speakers, the administrative staff of the program should prepare and distribute literature on this subject. Some of this literature is referenced in the suggested resources list at the back of this book. We encourage you to supplement this material with your own research and information. After reviewing the literature, have a focused discussion on the materials, evaluating their applicability to the curriculum.

To accomplish Objective 5, review the following discussion of group facilitation and teaching strategies. Enhance this discussion with some of your own experiences as an educator. Clarify how these strategies relate to the information you have just discussed. Continue to keep these strategies in mind as you move on to the fifth objective.

To realize Objective 6, hand out copies of this book and walk through the curriculum, paying particular attention to the teaching strategies, Africentric elements, and objectives for each session.

A sample *mzee* training session schedule for a one-day meeting follows. You will notice that it includes activities from the curriculum and allows *mzee* trainees to learn as they do.

Morning

9:15	Sign-in/introductions
9:45	*Durara umoja* (unity circle)* and *tambiko* (libations)*
10:00	Icebreaker activity or team-building activity
10:30	Presentation by cultural specialist
11:00	Working with African American adolescent males (see suggested resources)

Afternoon

12:15	Lunch
12:45	Team-building activity (any activity selected from the curriculum)
1:15	Distribution of *Brothers of Ujima* curriculum (copies of this book) and session-by-session overview
	Overview of *mzee* responsibilities
3:00	Questions and answers
	Closing remarks

Please refer to Session 1 for description of terms marked with an asterisk.

Mzee Group Facilitation and Teaching Strategies

A cooperative teaching style works best for *mzees*. This style helps manage group dynamics and models positive, productive, and respectful behavior for the boys. Be supportive, objective, and nonjudgmental. Practicing nonjudgment is key during sessions in which the boys share information or opinions that you may not have anticipated. The guidelines described next expand upon the cooperative teaching style.

Be prepared

Know the session! Read through the entire curriculum first. Several days in advance, make sure you have arranged all materials and confirmed any speakers. Then, at least two days before the session, review the session. If need be, make a few notes to keep handy during the session. Many sessions offer optional activities. Be prepared should the unexpected occur (e.g., a speaker cancels at the last minute).

Be yourself

As one facilitator put it, "Teens can spot a phony a mile away." And you'd better believe they're not going to be open and honest if you're not. On this same note, if you don't know the answer to a question, say so. Tell the boys that you will have the answer at the next session. Then keep your word. Doing this teaches the boys that they don't have to know everything either, but they can find out.

Be respectful

Again, be supportive, objective, and nonjudgmental. Treat the boys as you would want to be treated.

Be clear

Clarify abstract or vague language and terms. Since the *Brothers of Ujima* program is Africentric, the boys will often need clear definitions of terms. Learn this information. The glossary and suggested resources list at the back of this book are provided specifically for this purpose.

Be positive in the face of the negative

When a participant is practicing misbehavior, separate the person from the behavior. Instead of saying, "Please stop . . ." or "Don't . . ." remind the boy of what he agreed to do according to the group's rules. State this information clearly, referring to the rule.

Recognize positive behavior

If you are going to address misbehavior, you must also acknowledge positive behavior. Keeping the scale balanced shows the boys that the *mzees* are fair. It also empowers the boys to make decisions about how they want to be recognized—for positive behavior or misbehavior.

Ask open-ended questions

Open-ended questions allow boys the space to express themselves and articulate their perspectives, as opposed to merely agreeing or disagreeing with another's point of view. When brainstorming, make sure you get all responses before moving on with the session (interpreting, classifying, clarifying).

Practice active listening

Active listeners are more aware of group dynamics moment to moment. Thus, they are more able to facilitate. When implementing sessions, give the boys your full attention. Make eye contact. Paraphrase their responses and reflect their feelings. Recognize sincere replies and responses. Validate all feelings. Use open and inviting body language. Don't be afraid of silence. Sometimes it takes a moment or two for the boys to reflect on the question or to let information sink in.

Work to include all group members

Every group has a mix of personalities. Take the time to gently engage shy or withdrawn boys. Smile. Ask them, "How do you feel about that?" or "What do you think?" On the other end of the spectrum, some boys will be very forthcoming and vocal. Make sure that everyone receives equal attention and balanced responses. Also make sure that group members speak one at a time, beginning their statements with "I."

Be consistent

The ritualistic elements of the program (like the *durara umoja* and *tambiko*) provide needed structure and reinforcement. It is also important for *mzees* to provide transitions and closure when necessary. Thank the boys for their responses and whatever else they have provided that day. Let them know in advance when you are going to end an activity.

Enlist the support of other staff

When necessary, don't be afraid to rely upon your own peers to help during a difficult session. Model collaborative problem solving using a co-facilitator. Debrief with other session leaders after the session to develop new options for handling difficult and complex problems.

SESSION COMPONENTS AND MATERIALS

The session plans following this Facilitator's Guide provide specific guidelines for conducting the group meetings.

Session Components

Each session plan includes objectives, a list of necessary materials and explanation of any additional preparations that might be required, and a step-by-step description of the procedures. Suggested websites are provided in some sessions. These change over time, and those implementing the curriculum may have to search for updated information and links. Sessions are structured in the following way.

Opening rituals

Opening rituals include having the group gather together to form the *durara umoja* (circle of unity) and perform the *tambiko* (libations, or pouring of water on the earth).

Jamaa *work*

Following the opening rituals, the boys go to their separate *jamaas* to discuss and engage in activities relating to the *nguzo* (principle) and proverb of the day. As a part of *jamaa* work, the boys receive a loose-leaf binder and pages that include questions for discussion and individual responses. These pages, which may be photocopied from Appendix A, make up the *Brothers of Ujima Journal*. The boys also receive a *Staying in Focus* assignment to do before the next session.

In addition to working in their individual *jamaas*, the boys often come together to participate in larger discussion groups and large-group activities involving guest speakers.

Closing rituals

At the end of each session, the whole group comes together to re-form the *durara umoja* and to recite the *Brothers of Ujima Creed*. Snacks and informal discussion among *mzees* and participants conclude the session.

Program Materials

Besides an appropriate space, willing participants, and committed program facilitators and group leaders, the *Brothers of Ujima* program requires the following materials:

- A CD player and CD of African percussion music (music can also be played on an MP3 player, computer, or other electronic device)
- A large map of Africa
- A potted plant and pitcher to hold water for the *tambiko*
- Easel pads (one per *jamaa*)
- Poster board and markers
- Small loose-leaf binders (one per participant, to make the *Brothers of Ujima Journals*)
- A three-hole punch (to drill holes in the journal pages and handouts)
- Card stock (for photocopying the *Staying in Focus* assignments)
- Paper and pencils or pens
- Snacks to serve at the end of each session

Appendix B includes full-page versions of the *Brothers of Ujima Creed*, the Eight Principles for African-American Living (*Nguzo Nane*), and the eight individual principles. If you wish, you can reproduce these pages as larger posters for display in the program space. A few additional materials are needed to conduct specific activities; these are listed with each session.

> *Several days before each session, the facilitating staff should meet for an hour to prepare materials and conduct any necessary administrative or implementation discussion. Speakers should be arranged several weeks in advance. It is crucial that facilitators review sessions before implementation and have all materials ready to go before the boys arrive! Splitting your attention between setting up and trying to engage a group of arriving boys may present challenges.*

BROTHERS OF UJIMA PROGRAM AT A GLANCE

Program type

Africentric cultural enrichment for adolescent males

Objectives

- To help students gain an understanding of the *Nguzo Nane* (Eight Principles for Living)
- To increase knowledge of and appreciation for African and African American culture
- To encourage pursuit of physical health and fitness
- To encourage critical awareness of myths and stereotypes of African Americans presented in the media
- To develop creative thinking and leadership skills
- To strengthen personal goal setting and commitment to education
- To develop positive ways of coping and handling conflict
- To increase knowledge of local community history
- To increase awareness of adult role models within the African American community

Guiding principles

The Eight Principles for African American Living (*Nguzo Nane*)

Implementation

- Stand-alone or in conjunction with a complementary program (for example, tutoring, conflict resolution, sports program, or substance abuse prevention)
- Number of sessions: 14 (plus two additional optional sessions)
- Session duration: 2 hours

Target group

African American (or other open and interested) boys, ages 10 to 14

Group structure

At least one facilitator (*mzee*) for each group (*jamaa*) of eight boys

Facilitator characteristics

African American males 19 years or older. These could include other males of African descent.

Session environment

A large room with few distractions (windowless or covered windows, no foot traffic)

Session components

Opening and closing rituals, discussion, guest speakers, team-building activities, journaling, *Staying in Focus* activities, intellectual and cooperative challenges, and African and African American history and culture

Optional activities

Field trips to local, regional, and national cultural sites and resources, Kwanzaa celebration

SESSION PLANS

SESSION 1

Orientation

OBJECTIVES

- To provide an overview of the project, including the expectations, vocabulary, structures, and rules
- To help *mzees* and participants get to know each other

MATERIALS

Music player and recorded drumming or African percussion music

Pencils or pens

Name tags

Water and plant or soil for the *tambiko*

Copies of the journal cover page and *Brothers of Ujima Creed* (Appendix A, pages 135–136)

PREPARATION

- Create posters of the *Nguzo Nane (Eight Principles)* and the *Brothers of Ujima Creed*. Display these posters and a large map of Africa during this and all following sessions. If you wish, you can also create posters of the individual *Nguzo*/Principles for display in the larger group. Full-page examples of these materials are included in Appendix B.
- *Note*: Parents can be invited to attend part of the first session.

PROCEDURE

Before students arrive start the music.

Sign-In

As the boys arrive, have the *mzees* direct them to a table where they will sign in and make a nametag. *Mzees* not assigned to the sign-in table will greet students and engage them in initial conversation, asking their names and where they go to school, and introducing them to other young men or *mzees*. (*Note*: Be observant. Keep an eye out for introverted or shy youth and make an effort to keep them engaged, but don't overdo it.) Music or drumming continues to play during this time.

Program Introduction

1. Turn off the music or drumming and gather everyone together in a circle. Have the *mzees* spread themselves throughout the circle. Do not hold hands at this time.
2. The lead facilitator/senior *mzee* gives a brief overview of the program, covering expectations, attendance, and a brief description of some of the session topics. If parents are in attendance, their questions can be answered at this time. The script below can be used or modified to explain the program.

   > "The Brothers of Ujima program was developed for teens such as yourself. It is our hope that this program will support you in your transition from boyhood to manhood. You will learn about your heritage and about Africa and African Americans. You will also learn some of the challenges African American boys and men face, along with ways of addressing these challenges. We expect that you will behave according to the rules that will be discussed. It is important that you attend every session. Some of the topics we will cover include Africa, education, and being a brother-keeper for each other. We will also have guest speakers at some of the sessions."

3. Next, *mzees* explain the cultural elements of the program, describing the roles in African culture of the *mzee*, the *durara umoja*, and the *tambiko*, and introducing the *Nguzo Nane*. (Refer to the glossary at the end of this book for literal meanings and pronunciations of these words.)

4. Answer questions at this time, instructing students to introduce themselves by name when asking questions.
5. *Mzees* will then introduce the "call and response" signal that will be used to get the attention of the group. Explain that the words to be used are from the Twi language of the Akan peoples of Ghana, West Africa: *agoo*, roughly translated as "Attention," and *amee*, "I am listening."

Opening Ritual

- Have the members of the group hold hands to form the *durara umoja*. Some of the boys may be shy about holding hands, so do not force it. Parents may participate in this part of the program if they choose, but they should then leave.
- Remind the boys of the purpose and significance of the *durara umoja*. Have boys and *mzees* go around the circle to introduce themselves and share one thing for which they are thankful.
- Perform the *tambiko* (libation) by pouring water on the plant. *Mzee* walks around the group to allow each youth to pour the libation (to support youth engagement and participation).

Icebreaker Activity

Youth are introduced to and play Mancala.

Mancala is one of the oldest games in the world and can be easily played with whatever medium happens to be around. For example, African people often play using pebbles, small seashells, or seeds, with specially carved wooden boards or even directly on the ground. Variations of this mathematical game are played all over Africa and in other countries. See http://www.tradgames.org.uk/games/Mancala.htm for further information.

Directions

- Mancala is played with seven pits—six playing pits plus one score pit, the Kalaha—per player. At the beginning of the game, each of the 12 playing pits contains three seeds (or beads, stones, or balls).
- To play, the player chooses one playing pit from which to "sow" the seeds. Each seed in the pit is then placed, one at

a time, into the successive pits, moving counter-clockwise around the board.

- Seeds placed in a Kalaha are points for that player. Seeds are not sown in the opponent's Kalaha. If the last seed in a play is placed in the player's own Kalaha, he gets another turn. If the last seed is placed in an empty pit on the player's own side of the board, then he captures the seeds in the opposite (his opponent's) pit. All captured seeds, as well as the capturing piece, are placed in the player's Kalaha.
- The game ends when all of the playing pits on one side of the board are empty. The player with seeds remaining in his playing pits gets to put them into his Kalaha. The winner is the player with the most seeds in his Kalaha.

Note: another icebreaker activity or game can replace this one. Make sure the activity is one that involves all boys.

Closing Ritual

- The eldest *mzee* will call the group to order using the call and response method.
- Refer students to the poster of *Brothers of Ujima Creed,* and hand out copies of the creed. Standing, everyone reads it together. Ask for a student volunteer to lead the reading next session.
- Tell the boys that the next session's activity will involve forming family workgroups.

Share the snacks. Mzees should use this opportunity to chat informally with all of the boys. Encourage everyone to help clean up.

SESSION 2

Jamaa Building: Purpose, Introductions, and Rules

The journey begins . . . Sankofa!

OBJECTIVES

- To create individual *jamaas* or groups, and to begin to establish an emotionally safe atmosphere within them
- To begin building cohesion among participants
- To help students begin to gain an understanding of the *Nguzo Nane* (Eight Principles for Living)

MATERIALS

Music player and recorded drumming or music

Water and plant for the *tambiko*

Pencils or pens

Journals (loose-leaf binders, one per participant) and copies of the cover page and Session 2 journal page (Appendix A, pages 135 and 137)

Copies of the *Possible Jamaa Names* and *African Tribal and Ethnic Groups* handouts (optional, pages 34 and 35)

Easel pads and markers (one for each *jamaa*)

Map of Africa

Staying in Focus assignment cards for Session 2 (page 36)

Snacks

PREPARATION

- Determine how many *jamaas* you will need and decide on a way to assign participants to each (see the suggested activity). Assign one or more *mzees* to each *jamaa.*
- Prepare journals. Each journal should contain a cover page with the program name and a copy of the *Creed*.

PROCEDURE

Before the boys arrive, start the music. Continue to display the posters of the Nguzo Nane *(Eight Principles) and* Brothers of Ujima Creed, *along with the map of Africa.*

Opening Ritual

- Turn off the music. Gather everyone together for the *durara umoja*. *Mzees* should spread themselves throughout the circle. Remind students of its purpose and significance.
- Review the purpose of the *tambiko* and perform the libations.

Jamaa-Forming Activity

When forming jamaas, it is important to separate cliques and prevent last-minute switches as boys attempt to stay with their friends. Here is one procedure using index cards of different colors to create balanced group membership within jamaas.

- Create a stack of colored index cards based on how many *jamaas* you will need and how many boys will be in each *jamaa.* For example, if there will be three *jamaas* of eight boys each, you could use eight blue, green, and yellow cards (a total of 24). Alternate the colors—stacking first a blue card, then a green card, and finally a yellow card—until all 24 cards have been stacked.
- While the large group is still in the *durara umoja,* distribute the cards, being sure to rotate through the colors until all the cards have been given out. Boys having cards of the same color form a *jamaa.*
- Have the *mzees* collect their *jamaa* members, go to separate areas of the room, and sit in their own respective circles.

Jamaa Work

1. Circulate a sheet of paper and ask the members of your group to sign their names, then explain the purpose and function of the *jamaa*. *Jamaa* is a group or family (in this case, formed to help boys work together).
2. Naming the *jamaa*: Have the group name their *jamaa*. Ideas include having the boys choose from among the names of African nations or words on the *Possible Jamaa Names* and *African Tribal and Ethnic Groups* handouts. Have boys vote on the name that they feel will best describe their *jamaa*.
3. Conduct an introduction exercise: Have the students give their names and complete this statement: "One thing I can contribute to my *jamaa* is ________." This should be a positive quality. If a student has difficulty thinking of something, let him pass and come back to him at the end. If he continues to struggle, assist him. Make sure to reframe negatively worded statements. For example, instead of "I won't talk over others," encourage the boy to say, "I will practice listening to others."
4. Explain the purpose of rules/cultural norms to the group. For example, you could say, "In life we have rules for several reasons. Some of these reasons include: to help people feel safe, to observe and preserve culture, to create an environment where people feel respected." Give a concrete example of how a person might show respect.
5. Ask the group what rules they think the *jamaa* should have. Write these down on the easel pad. Only after the list has been completed, review and ask for clarification if necessary. Tell the group that many of the rules, such as respecting elders, speaking only positively about people, confidentiality, no fighting, etc., are *nonnegotiable,* meaning everyone must follow them. *Mzees* need to make sure these rules are included. Put an asterisk next to each necessary rule. Any remaining rules, such as "We should care for each other," are optional and may be adopted on an individual basis.
6. To show their willingness to abide by the rules, have members sign their names to the list. From now on a student should post the list at the start of each session.

7. Next, ask for two volunteers to write the *nguzo* (principle) and proverb for the session:

   Nguzo/Principle: Nia (Purpose)

   Proverb: "A paddle here, a paddle there, the canoe stays still."

   > *To be able to write the principle and proverb, volunteers will need something to refer to. Options for this and following sessions include giving them their journal page early and having them copy from that, or preparing and giving them separate index cards (the principle written on one, proverb written on the other).*

8. Have all the students practice pronouncing and saying the *nguzo*. Discuss the meaning of the proverb. Ask them how the proverb is related to the principle.

   Discussion Goals

   - Understanding the *nguzo* and proverb
   - Understanding the value of goals and purpose
   - Supporting and clarifying individual and group goal setting

   Discussion Questions

   - What does the word "purpose" mean?
   - Can you give me an example of someone with a purpose?
   - How can you tell if a person has purpose?
   - What does a person with purpose do?
   - What happens when a person lacks purpose?
   - How can (does) purpose play a role in your life?
   - What happens when more than one person is paddling, but not heading toward the same goal?
   - What needs to happen for people working together to get to their goals or achieve their purpose?

9. Hand out journals, pens or pencils, and the journal pages for Session 2. Have each boy fill out the title page and complete the journal page for Session 2. Point out that the journal includes a copy of the *Brothers of Ujima Creed* and let them know that they will be adding pages to their journals as the sessions continue. Ask if anyone has questions.

10. Collect the journals and pens or pencils and distribute the *Staying in Focus* cards for Session 2. Read the assignment on the card:

"Between now and the next session, practice two of your *jamaa* rules with your family or at school."

Answer any questions about the assignment and tell the boys that they should bring their cards to the next session and be ready to share their answers.

Closing Ritual

- Get the whole group's attention using the call and response method.
- Form the *durara umoja,* and have everyone read the *Brothers of Ujima Creed* together aloud.

Mention that the focus of the next session will be on physical health and ask the boys to wear comfortable clothes in which they can be active.

Share the snacks. Mzees should use this opportunity to chat informally with all of the boys. Encourage everyone to help clean up.

POSSIBLE JAMAA NAMES

Name	Pronunciation	Meaning	Origin
Bakari	(bah KAH ree)	Hopeful	Kiswahili
Amiri	(AH mee ree)	Leader	Kiswahili
Abiola	(ah BEE o lah)	Born in honor	Yoruba
Hondo	(HOHN do)	Warrior	Shona people (Zimbabwe)
Akinlana	(ah keen LAH nah)	Courage	Yoruba
Bomani	(bo MAH nee)	Warrior	Ngoni people (Malawi)
Chisulo	(chee SOO loh)	Strength of steel	Malawi
Minkah	(MEEN kah)	Justice	Akan people (Ghana)
Mwamba	(m WAM bah)	Strong, powerful	Tanzania
Olafemi	(ah lah FEH mee)	Successful	Yoruba
Sekou	(seh KOO)	Wise, educated	Guinea
Sentwali	(sehn TWAH lee)	Brave	Rwanda
Thabiti	(ta BEE tee)	A genuine man	Kenya
Umi	(OO me)	Energy	Malawi
Uuka	(oo OO kah)	Rise up	Xhosa (South Africa)
Zuberi	(zoo BEH ree)	Strong	Kiswahili

AFRICAN TRIBAL AND ETHNIC GROUPS

Ashanti: The Ashanti are a major ethnic group of the Akans in Ghana.

Bambara: The largest tribal group in Mali, many of the Bambara are farmers. They may live in large households, sometimes comprising 60 or more members.

Dogon: The Dogon are a cliff-dwelling people who live in southeastern Mali and Burkina Faso.

Fulani: The Fulani people of West Africa are the largest nomadic group in the world, primarily herders and traders.

Ibo: The Ibo people are from Nigeria. Traditionally they have lived in villages of a few hundred to thousands of people, comprising numerous extended families.

Mandinka: The Mandinka live in West Africa, primarily Senegal, The Gambia and Guinea-Bissau.

Masai: The Masai live on the plains of East Africa and are known as herders and warriors. The Masai believe in a single god, and their social structure is based on age groupings of males.

Wolof: Most modern members of this tribe live and work in urban areas in Senegal and are Muslim. Historically, the Wolof lived in villages that were run based on family leadership.

Xhosa: The Xhosa people are speakers of Bantu languages and live in southeastern South Africa.

Yoruba: The Yoruba people live in southwestern Nigeria and Benin. They have developed many forms of art, including pottery, weaving, beadwork, metalwork, and mask making.

Zulu: The Zulu people are the largest ethnic group in South Africa. They are known for their beads and baskets.

STAYING IN FOCUS ASSIGNMENT CARDS

Photocopy this page on card stock, then cut the cards apart (one card per participant).

SESSION 2: STAYING IN FOCUS

Between now and the next session, practice two of your *jamaa* rules with your family or at school.

SESSION 2: STAYING IN FOCUS

Between now and the next session, practice two of your *jamaa* rules with your family or at school.

SESSION 2: STAYING IN FOCUS

Between now and the next session, practice two of your *jamaa* rules with your family or at school.

SESSION 2: STAYING IN FOCUS

Between now and the next session, practice two of your *jamaa* rules with your family or at school.

SESSION 2: STAYING IN FOCUS

Between now and the next session, practice two of your *jamaa* rules with your family or at school.

SESSION 2: STAYING IN FOCUS

Between now and the next session, practice two of your *jamaa* rules with your family or at school.

SESSION 3

Health and Fitness

OBJECTIVES

- To increase boys' understanding of the benefits of a healthy lifestyle
- To increase boys' knowledge of how to access healthy recreational and physical fitness activities

MATERIALS

Music player and recorded African drumming or percussion music

Water and plant for the *tambiko*

Jamaas' rules posters from Session 2

Pencils or pens

Journals and copies of the Session 3 journal page (Appendix A, page 138)

Easel pads and markers for each *jamaa*

Appropriate space for physical activity

Other materials depending on speakers (e.g., jump ropes, cooking equipment, etc.)

Staying in Focus assignment cards for Session 3 (page 42)

Snacks

PREPARATION

- Tell the boys a week in advance to come dressed in comfortable clothing.

- Prepare a list of local places where boys can participate in health and physical activities (e.g., Boys and Girls Clubs, recreational facilities, faith-based youth programs, etc.). Make sure there are low- and no-cost alternatives.
- Arrange for participatory health and fitness activities (e.g., jumping rope, yoga, cooking healthy cultural dishes, African dance, *capoeira* or other martial arts). Plan more than one activity, and strive to expose boys to activities beyond those to which they have frequent exposure and access.
- Prepare speakers by providing them with information about the type of youth group, their participation and modeling in the *durara umoja*, the objectives for the session, and what they will provide (e.g., history of physical activity, benefits, etc.).
- Have demonstrations set up in separate stations.
- Ask speakers to structure their demonstrations to accommodate a range of comfort and participation levels among the boys.
- Review the suggested websites below to become familiar with health tips that can be shared with the boys.

Resource Sites

- http://www.nutrition.gov
- http://www.nlm.nih.gov/medlineplus/teenhealth.html
- http://www.cdc.gov/healthyyouth/healthtopics/index.htm
- http://www.cdc.gov/nccdphp/dnpao/index.html

PROCEDURE

Before the boys arrive, start the music. Continue to display the posters of the Nguzo Nane (Eight Principles) and Brothers of Ujima Creed, along with the map of Africa.

Opening Ritual

- Turn off the music. Gather everyone together for the *durara umoja*. *Mzees* should spread themselves throughout the circle. Ask the boys to explain the significance of the *durara umoja*.

- Perform the *tambiko*.

  Instruct the boys to get out their Staying in Focus cards and go to their jamaas.

Jamaa Work

1. Discuss the *Staying in Focus* assignment from the previous session by asking boys which *jamaa* rule they practiced.
2. Ask for three volunteers. Have one post the *jamaa's* rules poster and the other two write the *nguzo* (principle) and proverb of the day, respectively.

   Nguzo/Principle: Kujichagulia (Self-Determination)

   Proverb: "Disease and disasters come and go like rain, but health is like the sun that illuminates the entire village."

3. Have the boys practice saying and pronouncing the *nguzo* aloud. Discuss the meaning of the new proverb and how it relates to the *nguzo*.

   Discussion Goals

   - Understanding the *nguzo* and proverb
   - Understanding the value of health and physical activities
   - Supporting and clarifying individual and group health goals, activities, commitments, and responsibility (pointing out if necessary that each of us is responsible for our own health and well-being)

   Discussion Questions

   - What does it mean that health "illuminates the *entire* village?"
   - What does it mean to be healthy, and why is it important?
   - What can we do to be healthy?
   - How can people help one another in being healthy, and why is this important?

4. An *mzee* provides a brief discussion of the importance of healthy lifestyles. Ask the boys if they can identify some healthy lifestyle practices. Be sure to cover issues of:
   - Nutrition
   - Adequate sleep and rest

- Exercise and fitness (including concepts of endurance, strength, balance, and flexibility, and their importance)
- Avoiding risky behaviors

5. Assemble the boys in the larger group, using the call and response method. Introduce the guest presenters, and hold the presentation(s) or demonstration(s).

   If time and space allow, break boys up into two or more groups depending upon the number of participants. Participation should be voluntary and the demonstration organized so that those who are less fit or uncomfortable with public performance can have comfortable roles within the group and in the setting of the demonstration (e.g., by holding equipment or serving as an assistant).

6. Distribute the list of referrals for local physical fitness and health opportunities (including both food and exercise resources). Point out the variety and mix of individual and group opportunities. Note the importance of peers in supporting both individual and group fitness and make a specific connection to ideas of good sportsmanship.

   Have the boys return to their individual jamaa groups.

7. Have a discussion and public commitment by each youth as to what he can do to promote good physical health. Ask youth to be prepared to discuss one thing they can do over the next week to promote good physical health.
8. Hand out the journals and pencils or pens, and give each boy a copy of the journal page for Session 3. Read through it with them and ask if they have any questions. Have the boys complete the page.
9. Collect the journals and pens or pencils, and distribute the *Staying in Focus* cards for Session 3. Read the assignment on the card:

   "Select one thing your *jamaa* will do before the next session to practice good health and fitness. How will you help one another in achieving this?"

Answer any questions about the assignment, then tell the boys they should bring their cards to the next session and be ready to share their answers.

Closing Ritual

- Get the whole group's attention using the call and response method.
- Re-form the *durara umoja*, and have everyone read the *Brothers of Ujima Creed* together aloud.

  Share the snacks. Mzees should use this opportunity to chat informally with all of the boys. Encourage everyone to help clean up.

STAYING IN FOCUS ASSIGNMENT CARDS

Photocopy this page on card stock, then cut the cards apart (one card per participant).

SESSION 3: STAYING IN FOCUS

Select one thing your *jamaa* will do before the next session to practice good health and fitness. How will you help one another in achieving this?

SESSION 3: STAYING IN FOCUS

Select one thing your *jamaa* will do before the next session to practice good health and fitness. How will you help one another in achieving this?

SESSION 3: STAYING IN FOCUS

Select one thing your *jamaa* will do before the next session to practice good health and fitness. How will you help one another in achieving this?

SESSION 3: STAYING IN FOCUS

Select one thing your *jamaa* will do before the next session to practice good health and fitness. How will you help one another in achieving this?

SESSION 3: STAYING IN FOCUS

Select one thing your *jamaa* will do before the next session to practice good health and fitness. How will you help one another in achieving this?

SESSION 3: STAYING IN FOCUS

Select one thing your *jamaa* will do before the next session to practice good health and fitness. How will you help one another in achieving this?

SESSION 4

My Brother's Keeper

OBJECTIVES

- To assist the boys in learning to critically examine myths and stereotypes of African American males presented in the media
- To critically evaluate the boys' understanding of a "Thug Life" and introduce the concept of "My Brother's Keeper" to them

MATERIALS

Music player and recorded African drumming or percussion music

Water and plant for the *tambiko*

Jamaas' rules posters

Journals and copies of the Session 4 journal page (Appendix A, page 139)

Pencils or pens

Easel pads and markers for each *jamaa*

TV and DVD/VCR, or computer with internet connection

Copies of *100 Notable Black Men* handout (page 48)

Staying in Focus assignment cards for Session 4 (page 49)

Snacks

PREPARATION

- Identify a video clip or another depiction of negative stereotypical behavior such as excessive display of wealth, drug use, or misogyny (from a television program, music video, or film, YouTube, etc.). A positive one may be shown for contrast. Below are suggestions for positive and negative videos. You should also be able to find your own. Be sure to review the clips' appropriateness given the ages of the boys and local norms around the use of profanity.

- Music video, positive image: Talib Kweli, "Get By" (available on YouTube)
- Music video, negative image: The Diplomats featuring Cam'ron, Jim Jones, and Juelz Santana, "Crunk Muzik" (available on YouTube, including an edited version)

PROCEDURE

Before the boys arrive, start the music. Continue to display the posters of the Nguzo Nane (Eight Principles) and Brothers of Ujima Creed, along with the map of Africa.

Opening Ritual

- Turn off the music. Gather everyone together for the *durara umoja*. *Mzees* should spread themselves throughout the circle.
- Perform the *tambiko*.

Instruct the boys to get out their Staying in Focus assignment cards and go to their jamaas.

Jamaa Work

1. Ask for three volunteers. Have one post the *jamaa's* rules poster and the other two write the *nguzo* and proverb of the day.

   Nguzo/Principle: Umoja (Unity)

   Proverb: "When elephants jostle, what gets hurt is the grass."

2. Have all the students say the *nguzo*. Discuss the meaning of the proverb. Ask them to relate the proverb to the principle.

   Discussion Goals

   - Understanding the *nguzo* and proverb
   - Understanding the value of working together, of cooperation

- Supporting and clarifying individual and group commitments to unity and making good judgments of unity "investments" and mutual support

Discussion Questions

- Who might the elephants represent? Who could the grass represent?
- Reflect back on the *nguzo* and proverb from Session 2 (*Nia,* purpose): "A paddle here, a paddle there, the canoe stands still." How can unity and purpose be linked? How do you see unity and purpose linked in your community?
- Can you think of examples in your community where there is not unity? What happens?

3. Ask the boys, "With a show of hands and without saying what you did, who followed through on the *Staying in Focus* assignment from the last session?" Then ask if anyone would like to share what they did. Don't discuss their answers. Simply thank them for sharing. Ask youth to report on one thing they have done to promote their physical health or to help other members of their group.
4. Introduce the concept of "My Brother's Keeper." Ask the boys, "What does 'Thug Life' mean?"
5. Review the myths and stereotypes below. Incorporate a video clip, song, or any other form of media into the discussion.

Myths and Stereotypes

- Myth #1: African American men express their manhood by showing their individual physical toughness. They want to show how thug or gangsta they can be.
- Myth #2: African American men are violent and live violent lives.
- Myth #3: All African American men do is sell drugs and buy jewelry.
- Myth #4: African American men do not take care of their families.
- Myth #5: African American men are more interested in wealth than education.
- Myth #6: Most African American men have been in jail or prison.

Countering Stereotypes Discussion

- How are stereotypes established? How do they spread? Are these stereotypes true?
- What don't we see? Use news and other media examples, the list of *100 Notable Black Men* (on page 48 at end of this session), as well as data that reflect the many successes of African American men. *Mzees* may have the boys add to this list or search to identify additions (e.g., establish a list of *10 Local Notable Black Men*; see the optional assignment/activity below).
- To individual examples, ask, "Is [*name*] a man because he is tough? Is [*name*] violent? Does [*name*] sell drugs and buy jewelry?"
- What are the effects of the stereotypes? On you? On others?
- What can be done to counter or work against stereotypes? For yourself? For your brothers? For other members of your community?
- Can you change the minds of everybody? Should you try? What if you fail?

Optional Assignment/Activity

Working in teams, boys identify African American males who are making a positive difference in their community. These may be youth, local figures, or historical figures. *Mzees* may have compiled a list of local African American males who are willing to be interviewed (by phone or in person) about their lives and their positive contributions to the community. When identifying these individuals, take care to ensure they convey program values and make sure that contacts are established to support youth safety and appropriate adult boundaries (e.g., by having adults come to the program session to be interviewed, or by setting up adult-supervised interviews with pairs of boys).

---

6. Discuss this closing thought: "We as African American men are linked to each other through creation; by bringing or allowing harm to another, we are actually hurting each other. We have a spiritual and moral obligation to each other.

Regardless of where you live, what your financial situation is, or who your friends are, we are each other's keepers."

7. Hand out the journals and pencils or pens, and give each boy a copy of the journal page for Session 4. Read through it with them and ask if they have any questions. Have the boys complete the page.
8. Collect the journals and pens or pencils, then distribute the *Staying in Focus* assignment cards for Session 4.

   "Identify two African American men who have made an important contribution to their community. Learn something new about these men to share with your *jamaa.*"

   Read the assignment on the card and tell the boys that they should bring their cards to the next session and be ready to share their answers.

Closing Ritual

- Get the whole group's attention using the call and response method.
- Re-form the *durara umoja,* and have everyone read the *Brothers of Ujima Creed* together aloud.

  Share the snacks. Mzees use this opportunity to chat informally with all of the boys. Encourage everyone to help with clean-up.

100 NOTABLE BLACK MEN

Hank Aaron
Alvin Ailey
Muhammad Ali
Wally Amos
Louis Armstrong
Arthur Ashe
James Baldwin
Ernie Banks
Benjamin Banneker
Imamu Amiri Baraka
Ernie Barnes
Count Basie
Romare Bearden
Chuck Berry
John Biggers
Cory Booker
Tom Bradley
James Brown
Willie Brown
Ralph Bunche
Geoffrey Canada
George Washington Carver
Ray Charles
Nat King Cole
John Coltrane
Sean Combs
Countee Cullen
Miles Davis
David Dinkins
Frederick Douglass
Charles Richard Drew
W.E.B. DuBois
Paul Lawrence Dunbar
Michael Eric Dyson
Duke Ellington
Ralph Ellison
Julius Erving
John Hope Franklin
Joe Frazier
Marcus Garvey
Henry Louis Gates, Jr.
Berry Gordy
Jimi Hendrix
Matthew Henson
Langston Hughes
Kareem Abdul Jabbar
Jesse Jackson, Jr.
Maynard Jackson
Jack Johnson
James Weldon Johnson
John H. Johnson
Magic Johnson
Quincy Jones
Michael Jordan
Percy Julian
B.B. King
Martin Luther King, Jr.
Lewis Latimer
Jacob Lawrence
Spike Lee
Sugar Ray Leonard
Carl Lewis
Joe Louis
Thurgood Marshall
Wynton Marsalis
Willie Mays
Ronald McNair
Barack Obama
Jesse Owens
Gordon Parks
Tyler Perry
P.B.S. Pinchback
Alvin Poussaint
Colin Powell
A. Phillip Randolph
Paul Roberson
Bill "Bojangles" Robinson
Sugar Ray Robinson
Jackie Robinson
Dred Scott
Tupac Shakur
Robert Smalls
Tavis Smiley
Will Smith
Carl Stokes
Henry O. Tanner
Fats Waller
Booker T. Washington
Denzel Washington
Harold Washington
Muddy Waters
Cornel West
L. Douglas Wilder
August Wilson
Stevie Wonder
Richard Wright
Malcolm X
Andrew Young
Coleman Young
Whitney Young

STAYING IN FOCUS ASSIGNMENT CARDS

Photocopy this page on card stock, then cut the cards apart (one card per participant).

SESSION 4: STAYING IN FOCUS

Identify two African American men who have made an important contribution to their community. Learn something new about these men to share with your *jamaa*.

SESSION 4: STAYING IN FOCUS

Identify two African American men who have made an important contribution to their community. Learn something new about these men to share with your *jamaa*.

SESSION 4: STAYING IN FOCUS

Identify two African American men who have made an important contribution to their community. Learn something new about these men to share with your *jamaa*.

SESSION 4: STAYING IN FOCUS

Identify two African American men who have made an important contribution to their community. Learn something new about these men to share with your *jamaa*.

SESSION 4: STAYING IN FOCUS

Identify two African American men who have made an important contribution to their community. Learn something new about these men to share with your *jamaa*.

SESSION 4: STAYING IN FOCUS

Identify two African American men who have made an important contribution to their community. Learn something new about these men to share with your *jamaa*.

SESSION 5

Introduction to Africa and African Culture: Fact and Fiction

OBJECTIVES

- To gain an understanding of participants' feelings about and expand their knowledge of Africa
- To help boys increase their connection to Africa and people of African descent

MATERIALS

Music player and recorded African drumming or percussion music

Water and plant for the *tambiko*

Jamaas' rules posters

Journals and copies of the Session 5 journal page (Appendix A, page 140)

Pencils or pens

Computers with internet access

Copies of *Africa Facts* handout (pages 56–57)

Easel pads and markers for each *jamaa*

Staying in Focus assignment cards for Session 5 (page 58)

Snacks

PREPARATION

- Find and review a news clip or a magazine article about Africa.
- Review websites below for further information about Africa.

Web Resources

- http://www.nhm.org/africa/
- http://www.mnh.si.edu/africanvoices/
- http://www.pbs.org/wnet/africa/index.html
- http://www.pbs.org/wonders/
- http://www.bbc.co.uk/worldservice/specials/1624_story_of_africa/
- http://news.bbc.co.uk/cbbcnews/hi/newsid_4100000/newsid_4101000/4101060.stm
- http://travel.nationalgeographic.com/places/continents/continent_africa.html
- http://www.nationsencyclopedia.com/economies/Africa/index.html

PROCEDURE

Before the boys arrive, start the music. Continue to display the posters of the Nguzo Nane (Eight Principles) and Brothers of Ujima Creed, along with the map of Africa.

Opening Ritual

- Turn off the music. Gather everyone together for the *durara umoja*. *Mzees* should spread themselves throughout the circle. Ask the group to explain the significance of the *durara umoja*. If no one responds, remind the students of its purpose and significance.
- Perform the *tambiko*.

Instruct the boys to get out their Staying in Focus cards and go to their jamaas.

Jamaa Work

1. Ask for three volunteers. Have one post the *jamaa's* rules poster, and the other two write the *nguzo* and proverb of the day.

   Nguzo/Principle: Umoja (Unity)

   Proverb: "The ruin of a nation begins in the homes of its people."

2. Have all the students practice saying the *nguzo*. Discuss the meaning of the proverb and relate the proverb to the *nguzo*.

   Discussion Goals

   - Understanding the *nguzo* and proverb
   - Understanding the value of unity
   - Supporting and clarifying individual and group opportunities to support positive outcomes obtained through unity

   Discussion Questions

   - What does this proverb mean?
   - What nation do you think they are talking about?
   - What might happen in the homes of the people that might mean the ruin of a nation?
   - How can unity play a role in addressing/countering those challenges?

3. Check on the last session's *Staying in Focus* assignment. Have boys share what they learned about two African American men.
4. Introduce today's session by asking the boys if they can remember the last session related to *Umoja*. Remind them that they discussed myths and misperceptions of African American males. Discuss with boys the benefit of being able to identify information and images as myths, stereotypes, or misrepresentations. To do this, they must be able to think critically just as they did in that session
5. Engage the boys in a discussion around why as Americans of African descent, it is important that they learn about Africa, and that the next exercise will help them get started. Have the

boys put away their *Staying in Focus* cards, and hand out the journals and copies of the journal page for Session 5: "What do you think about Africa?" Tell the boys that you are going to take them through an exercise to see what different things they know and what they think about Africa. They will not have to turn in the paper, and they will not be graded. This is a learning exercise.

6. Ask the boys to write a brief response to each of the statements on the journal page. This is to be done individually, using their first thoughts. Encourage them to be honest and to use the first answer that comes to mind. Take them through this quickly without any discussion.
   - Africa is…
   - African people are…
   - When I hear the word "Africa" I think…
   - Africans probably think America is / Americans are…
   - Some things I would like to know about Africa are…
   - I would (or would not) like to visit Africa because…
7. Show a news video or hand out copies of an article about contemporary Africa. Distribute the *Africa Facts* handout about contemporary and historic contributions of Africans. Ask *jamaa* members to read parts of the fact sheet. If computers are available, set up computers to different websites and allow *jamaa* members 10 to 20 minutes to find out something new about Africa that they would like to share with the group. Each *jamaa* should prepare a 5-minute presentation of these new materials to support their own and their peers' learning.
8. Conduct a web search (e.g., Google News, Google Video) for additional information and sources on Africa. Discuss the importance of verifying information and sources ("Can you believe everything you hear?")
9. Have each *jamaa* group facilitate a discussion of the boys' discoveries and their journal entries. Begin by allowing *jamaa* members to present new pieces of information and what they thought about this information.
10. Next, ask members to share the responses to the first open-ended statement on the journal page. Write the responses down on the easel pad, but don't allow any discussion until

everyone who wants to share has had a chance to do so. Do this for each statement. Continue with each statement until you've completed the list. Do not allow them to criticize one another's statements. Validate the honesty of the responses.

11. Bring all *jamaa* groups together and facilitate a discussion. Note the similarities and differences between the fact sheet information and the boys' perceptions as reflected in their journal question responses. Why are there similarities? Why are there differences?
12. Discuss with the boys whether they think that people have very different and sometimes negative attitudes about Africa, perhaps because of the inaccurate, narrow, and often racist portrayals of Africa in movies and television programs.
13. Ask the boys, "As Americans of African descent, has this discussion affected how you think of yourselves? How?" Discuss their responses. Ask boys how they can continue to deepen their knowledge and understanding of Africa and Africans.
14. After the discussion, collect the journals and pens or pencils. Distribute the *Staying in Focus* assignment cards for Session 5:

    "Choose two countries in Africa. Learn something new about these countries to share with your *jamaa* at the next session."

    Read the instructions on the card and tell the boys that they should bring their cards to the next session and be ready to share their answers. Encourage them to help one other remember to bring their cards.

Closing Ritual

- Get the whole group's attention using the call and response method
- Re-form the *durara umoja*, and have everyone read the *Brothers of Ujima Creed* together aloud.

    Share the snacks. Mzees should use this opportunity to chat informally with all the boys. Encourage everyone to help with clean-up.

AFRICA FACTS

1. There are over 1,500 languages spoken in Africa.
2. About 25% of the world's languages are spoken in Africa.
3. Kiswahili is one of the more common languages spoken in Africa and is used as a trade language when English is not used.
4. There are 53 countries in Africa. Each country has its own culture, language, and customs.
5. Africa is currently the poorest and least developed of all the continents.
6. There are five major regions or geographical areas in Africa. These include Eastern Africa, which include Ethiopia, Somalia, and Rwanda; Middle Africa, which includes Cameroon, Angola, and Congo; Western Africa, which includes Nigeria, Ghana, and Senegal; Southern Africa, which includes South Africa, Namibia, and Botswana; and Northern Africa, which includes Egypt, Sudan, and Tunisia.
7. Africa is second to Asia in the number of people that live there. About one billion people live in Africa.
8. About half of the worlds' diamonds come from Africa.
9. Nigeria is the most populated country in Africa and the 8th largest country in the world.
10. English is the main language spoken in Nigeria.
11. Football (soccer) is Nigeria's national sport.
12. Rugby is the most popular sport in South Africa.
13. South Africa is popular among tourists with close to 900,000 visitors a month.

14. Robben Island holds the prison where Nelson Mandela was imprisoned for 18 of his 27 years in prison. It is a popular tourist attraction.
15. Kenya is known for its champion long distance runners. Football (soccer) and cricket are other popular sports.
16. Kenya is known for producing tea and coffee.
17. The Nile is the longest river in the world. Some of the African countries it runs through are Tanzania, Uganda, Sudan, and Egypt.
18. Zimbabwe has the highest adult literacy rate of any African country at over 90%.
19. Liberia in West Africa was founded by freed American and Caribbean slaves.
20. African immigrants to the United States are likely to come from Nigeria, Ghana, and Ethiopia.

STAYING IN FOCUS ASSIGNMENT CARDS

Photocopy this page on card stock, then cut the cards apart (one card per participant).

SESSION 5: STAYING IN FOCUS

Choose two countries in Africa.
Learn something new about these countries to share with your *jamaa* at the next session.

SESSION 5: STAYING IN FOCUS

Choose two countries in Africa.
Learn something new about these countries to share with your *jamaa* at the next session.

SESSION 5: STAYING IN FOCUS

Choose two countries in Africa.
Learn something new about these countries to share with your *jamaa* at the next session.

SESSION 5: STAYING IN FOCUS

Choose two countries in Africa.
Learn something new about these countries to share with your *jamaa* at the next session.

SESSION 5: STAYING IN FOCUS

Choose two countries in Africa.
Learn something new about these countries to share with your *jamaa* at the next session.

SESSION 5: STAYING IN FOCUS

Choose two countries in Africa.
Learn something new about these countries to share with your *jamaa* at the next session.

SESSION 6

African and African American Culture: Yesterday and Today

OBJECTIVES

- To increase knowledge and appreciation of African and African American culture
- To increase the boys' sense of connection to Africa and African people

MATERIALS

Music player and recorded African drumming or percussion music

Water and plant for the *tambiko*

Jamaas' rules posters

Journals and copies of journal page for Session 6 (Appendix A, page 141)

Pencils or pens

Copies of the *Africa: Historical and Current Facts* and *African Kings and Leaders* handouts (pages 64–67)

Staying in Focus assignment cards for Session 6 (page 68)

Snacks

PREPARATION

- Obtain 10 photographs of modern Africa for each *jamaa*. Use personal photographs, reference books, posters from travel agencies, and other resources. The photographs should include political, economic, and social leaders and a variety of locations.

PROCEDURE

Before the boys arrive, start the music. Continue to display the posters of the Nguzo Nane (Eight Principles) and Brothers of Ujima Creed, along with the map of Africa.

Opening Ritual

- Turn off the music. Gather everyone together for the *durara umoja*. *Mzees* should spread themselves throughout the circle. Ask the group to explain the significance of the *durara umoja*.
- Perform the *tambiko*.

Instruct the boys to get out their Staying in Focus assignment cards and go to their jamaas.

Jamaa Work

1. Ask for three volunteers. Have one post the *jamaa's* rules poster and the other two write the *nguzo* and proverb of the day.

   Nguzo/Principle: Umoja (Unity)

   Proverb: "A people without knowledge of its history is like a tree without roots."

2. Have the students practice saying the *nguzo*. Discuss the meaning of the proverb and relate the proverb to the *nguzo*.

   Discussion Goals

   - Understanding the *nguzo* and proverb
   - Understanding the value of unity
   - Supporting and clarifying individual and group opportunities to support positive outcomes obtained through unity

Discussion Questions

- What does this proverb mean?
- What function do roots play for a tree? What happens when a tree doesn't have roots? How can knowledge serve as "roots" for a group of people?
- If necessary, point out that unity increases when knowledge about how all people from Africa are linked increases.

3. Announce to the boys that this session will continue on the topic of Africa. Begin by discussing the last session's *Staying in Focus* assignment:

   "Choose two countries in Africa. Learn something new about these countries to share with your *jamaa* at the next session."

   Ask for volunteers to share their responses.

   If some students are not prepared, ask the group to come up with an effective way to help each other be better prepared for the next session. Write down their solution.

4. Talk with the boys about the ways that impressions of Africa or the history of African Americans have frequently been shaped by people who weren't of African descent. The boys can consider the analogy of a stranger, who may not even like them, going on television and telling the whole world about them. Would that person give a fair and honest picture of who they are? Point out that many things they may have seen or heard about Africa are told by people who weren't African.
5. Note that not only is Africa the homeland to all African Americans just as Ireland is homeland to Irish Americans and China is the homeland to Chinese Americans, but that the first humans lived in Africa. Remnants of the earliest humans, dating back millions of years, were found in East Africa.
6. Explain to the boys that symbols used in the United States are of African origin. As an example, draw an obelisk on the easel pad and ask the boys if they can think of a famous monument that resembles your drawing. (The answer is the Washington Monument.) The symbol of the healing professions, snakes around a staff, called the *caduceus*, was also taken from Africa. The aviator wings of commercial and military pilots come from the ancient Kemetic symbol of the soul.

7. Explain that historians call Africa the "Cradle of Civilization," and that many "firsts" originated in Africa. For example, it is considered the home to the first university in the world (Al-Azhar University in Cairo, Egypt), and to the studies of mathematics and astronomy. Distribute the *Africa: Historical and Current Facts* handout. Have the boys take turns reading the facts and encourage them to try and pronounce the words that are unfamiliar to them.
8. Distribute the *African Kings and Leaders* handout. Ask the boys if they've heard of any of them. Briefly talk about each of the kings in terms of their character, strength, and leadership. Help the boys see that African kings were examples of true leaders. They were mentally tough, physically strong, and politically shrewd. They ruled with fairness and strength, and they did what it took to help their people survive, even going to war if necessary.
9. Announce to the boys that they are now going to see a different Africa than what is usually shown on television and in the movies. Show the boys the photographs or websites of modern Africa that show urban development, rich natural resources, and diversity of cultures and people. Point out that modern Africa has large cities, airports, advanced telecommunication systems such as cell phones and Internet, office buildings, and great artists and musicians. Remind them that Africa is the second largest continent in land area, and is several times larger than the United States—the continental United States would fit into Africa's Sahara Desert. Ask them which continent has the world's largest reserves of diamonds and gold. (Answer: Africa)

Optional Activity

Bring the *jamaas* together for a presentation by a cultural specialist. This person can be a staff member or an invited guest who will discuss some aspect of African culture. For example, an agent from a travel agency may be invited, a professor of African history from a local university, or a person from Africa.

---

10. Conclude by saying that all countries have strengths and weaknesses. For example, here in the United States there is a great deal of material wealth. On the other hand, millions of Americans are homeless. Identify for them (or ask them to identify) some of the strengths and weaknesses of the countries of Africa. Point out that most countries in Africa have had independence for fewer than 50 years. Discuss with them how these countries fought for their independence, defeating colonial powers with strong leadership, commitment, and sacrifice. Remind them that *all* countries have strengths and weaknesses.
11. Hand out the journals and pens or pencils, and distribute copies of the journal page for Session 6. Read through the journal page together, and ask if anyone has any questions. Have the boys complete the journal page.
12. Collect the journals and pencils. Distribute the *Staying in Focus* assignment cards for Session 6.

    "Share one new thing you have learned about Africa with someone who is not in the *Brothers of Ujima* program."

    Read the instructions on the card and tell the boys that they should bring their cards to the next session and be ready to share their answers. Encourage them to help one another remember to bring their cards.

Closing Ritual

- Get the whole group's attention using the call and response method.
- Re-form the *durara umoja*, and have everyone read the *Brothers of Ujima Creed* together aloud.

    Share the snacks. Mzees should use this opportunity to chat informally with all the boys. Encourage everyone to help with clean-up.

AFRICA: HISTORICAL AND CURRENT FACTS

Historical Facts

- Egypt is a country in Northeast Africa. Its original name was Kemet, which means "the black land." It was the center of the world's earliest and greatest civilization.
- Imhotep, who lived in ancient Egypt, is recognized as the first man of science in recorded history and the world's first doctor.
- The greatest pyramid in the world is located in Egypt. Pyramids are huge stone structures, square at the bottom with four triangular sides whose points meet at the top. The Great Pyramid of Giza is the only one of the Seven Wonders of the Ancient World that survives.
- Hieroglyphics were the writing system of the ancient Egyptians. Symbols and pictures were used to represent words. The modern-day alphabet evolved from this system.
- Arithmetic and other forms of mathematics were developed in Kemet and used to make statues and pyramids.
- Al-Azhar University in Cairo, Egypt, is considered to be the oldest university in the world. It was founded roughly the same time as the city of Cairo, in 969 AD. The first lecture was delivered in 975 AD.
- Many African symbols are highly respected throughout the world. For example, the Washington Monument is a symbol of an obelisk that was built in early Ethiopia.
- Many developments affecting the rest of Africa took place in or near the Nile Valley, such as the cultivation of plants and the development of metal smelting.

Current Facts

- Africa is the second largest continent in land area in the world and is over three times the size of the United States.
- Africa has 53 countries in five regions: North Africa, West Africa, Central Africa, East African, and Southern Africa.
- Africa has many thriving cities with airports, modern transportation systems, high-rise buildings, businesses, cultural events, and art.
- Major cities include Johannesburg, South Africa; Lagos, Nigeria; Accra, Ghana; Dakar, Senegal; Lusaka, Republic of Zambia; Nairobi, Kenya; Cairo, Egypt; and Addis-Ababa, Ethiopia.
- Although the majority of the population of Africa lives in rural areas, about one third live in cities.
- Over 1,500 different languages are spoken in Africa by diverse ethnic groups, each with its own traditions, customs, and way of life. Kiswahili is one of the more widely spoken African languages. It is spoken by more than 20 million people.
- People in Africa practice different religions. Most people practice Christianity or Islam. Fewer people practice traditional African religion.

AFRICAN KINGS AND LEADERS

Imhotep (c. 2980 B.C.)

Imhotep was an Egyptian priest who was the first multi-genius in recorded history. He was also an engineer and the first physician to emerge from ancient history. Imhotep is reputed to have designed the step pyramid in Egypt. He was also known to be a poet and philosopher, and was a writer of proverbs, one of which was: "Eat, drink and be merry, for tomorrow we may die."

Akhenaten (c. 1350 B.C.)

Akhenaten was an Egyptian pharaoh who was the first individual in recorded history to declare the existence of one God. Therefore, he is known as the father of monotheism, which is the key religious belief of Judaism, Christianity, and Islam. Although his father, Amenophis III, and great grandfather, Thotmes III, were powerful conquerors who built kingdoms of great wealth, Akhenaten devoted his life to art, literature, and knowledge. He continued the Egyptian tradition of building temples and colossal statues. However, his religious and philosophical views were considered extremely radical. After his death at the age of 31, his successors quickly re-established many of the conservative religious beliefs and institutions that Akhenaten had attempted to reform.

Hannibal of Carthage (247–183 B.C.)

Hannibal was perhaps the greatest military strategist of all time. At the age of 26 he led his army, with elephants, across the Alps to deliver a stunning defeat of the Romans. Many of his tactics are still taught as part of military training in the United States and other parts of the world.

Kafur the Magnificent (A.D. 967)

Kafur was a eunuch and slave who rose to be de-facto ruler of Egypt as guardian of the late sultan's young sons. He was described as being "deep shiny black," and was reputed to be overweight and to have walked "like a walrus." After years of being despised, he impressed the sultan with his character and was given an opportunity to prove himself in battle, where he achieved several significant military victories. As a leader he restored Egypt to a high level of military power. He also devoted time to the cultivation of the arts and sciences. He demonstrated religious tolerance by appointing a Jew to a high position in his court. He was known for his generosity and justice and was perhaps the first of a long dynasty of Mamluks, slave kings.

Sonni Ali (A.D. 1493)

Sonni Ali was a Muslim emperor of the vast Songhay empire that stretched from the Atlantic Ocean to the borders of modern Sudan. In addition to great wealth, Songhay was the site of the University of Timbuktu, the world's premier learning institution. Sonni Ali was known to have provided military support that protected the Jews, especially those residing in Europe, from persecution by the Christians. He reigned with great justice and generosity. It was told that an individual could walk from one end of the kingdom to another and not be harmed in any way. Crime was almost unknown and the people lived in peace. Several writers attributed this virtually crime-free condition to Sonni Ali's preference for severe punishment of minor infractions.

STAYING IN FOCUS ASSIGNMENT CARDS

Photocopy this page on card stock, then cut the cards apart (one card per participant).

SESSION 6: STAYING IN FOCUS

Share one new thing you have learned about Africa with someone who is not in the *Brothers of Ujima* program.

SESSION 6: STAYING IN FOCUS

Share one new thing you have learned about Africa with someone who is not in the *Brothers of Ujima* program.

SESSION 6: STAYING IN FOCUS

Share one new thing you have learned about Africa with someone who is not in the *Brothers of Ujima* program.

SESSION 6: STAYING IN FOCUS

Share one new thing you have learned about Africa with someone who is not in the *Brothers of Ujima* program.

SESSION 6: STAYING IN FOCUS

Share one new thing you have learned about Africa with someone who is not in the *Brothers of Ujima* program.

SESSION 6: STAYING IN FOCUS

Share one new thing you have learned about Africa with someone who is not in the *Brothers of Ujima* program.

SESSION 7

What I Bring to My Community

OBJECTIVES

- To assist boys in identifying and developing creative thinking and leadership skills that can be used in the local community
- To foster knowledge and a sense of respect for the community in which the boys live

MATERIALS

Music player and recorded African drumming or percussion music

Water and plant for the *tambiko*

Jamaas' rules posters

Easel pads and markers for each *jamaa*

Journals and copies of the Session 7 journal page (Appendix B, page 142)

Staying in Focus assignment cards for Session 7 (page 77)

Snacks

PREPARATION

- Prepare a list of local people in the community who have made a difference in the African American community
- Generate a list of potential community projects that can be carried out in a short period of time (ideally, single events or

projects that can be completed within the time frame of the ongoing program). Contact community agencies and groups (e.g., local cultural groups, United Way, National Urban League, local volunteer coordinating organizations).

PROCEDURE

Before the boys arrive, start the music. Continue to display the posters of the Nguzo Nane (Eight Principles) and Brothers of Ujima Creed, along with the map of Africa.

Opening Ritual

- Turn off the music. Gather everyone together for the *durara umoja*. *Mzees* should spread themselves throughout the circle
- Perform the *tambiko*.

Instruct the boys to get out their Staying in Focus assignment cards and go to their jamaas.

Jamaa Work

1. Ask for three volunteers. Have one post the *jamaa's* rules poster, and the other two write the *nguzo* and proverb of the day.

   Nguzo/Principle: Ujamaa (Cooperative Economics)

   Proverb: "Let not what you cannot do tear from your hands what you can do."

2. Have the students practice saying the *nguzo*. Discuss the meaning of the proverb and relate the proverb to the *nguzo*.

   Discussion Goals

   - Understanding the *nguzo* and proverb
   - Understanding the value of working together and shared responsibility for economic and financial well-being
   - Supporting and clarifying individual and group opportunities to work together and to understand the link between important individual efforts and the power of group efforts

Discussion Questions

- What does this proverb mean?
- What kinds of changes could happen to make the United States (or your local community) a better place to live? What can each of you as individuals do to make that happen? What could your *jamaa* do? What if you could get all the African American males in the city—what could they do as a group? What can a group accomplish that an individual cannot?
- What are the different things that people bring or exchange in their community? Is it only money? What other important resources do people bring to their communities?
- What if 30 million people (i.e., all African Americans) gave 50 cents? What is the danger of just focusing on what people exchange in terms of money?
- What happens if the individual does not do his part or if everyone thinks, "My part is so small, what can I do?" Note the importance of what one individual can do and the power that comes from many people working together.

3. Begin by discussing the last session's *Staying in Focus* assignment:

   "Share one thing you've learned about Africa with someone not in the *Brothers of Ujima* program."

   Ask the boys who they had talked to about Africa and what they had talked about. Get responses from three or four boys.
4. Continue with a discussion of how youth can impact and make a difference within the community. Discuss positive community leaders, local and nationally, and how they have benefited the community.
5. Assemble the boys into the larger group, then let them know that they will be forming new groups of 10 to 12 members each to participate in a team-building activity. To form these groups, you can have the boys count off from 1 to 3 (or 4, depending on the number of boys).

Team-Building Activity: Underground Railroad

In this activity, a group (ideally 10 to 12 participants) must travel from a designated starting point to a designated destination. The challenge is that group members have limited resources to make the trip. Resources are represented by carpet squares, and the journey takes place from station to station. These stations are areas the same size as the carpet squares, marked with masking tape on the floor and approximately 36 inches apart. This distance is only a suggestion. The idea is to make it challenging but not impossible for the boys to move between stations. Also remember to closely monitor the activity at all times in order to ensure the physical and emotional safety of all participants.

Background

To get started, find out what the group knows about the Underground Railroad. If necessary, explain that the Underground Railroad was a system by which many people of African heritage escaped from slave states in the South to freedom in the North and Canada. They traveled at night with very little in the way of personal belongings and food. Abolitionists often assisted by establishing "stations" along the route where the escaping slaves could temporarily rest, receive food, and get useful information.

Directions

1. Explain to the group that they are a family traveling from one safe house or station to another and that everyone must go together, as a unit. No one may be left behind. Tell them there will be dangers on their journey as they travel but that they will be given a few resources for their journey.
2. Distribute carpet squares among the group and tell the group that these squares represent resources such as food, water, and one or two cherished possessions. These resources—along with their cooperation, trust in one another, determination, and faith—will aid them in making the journey.

3. Explain that the group must stand only on the carpet squares as they travel to their destination and that some part of their body must always be in contact with the squares. If a resource (square) is not being used (in physical contact with a group member), it will be taken away (forfeited) immediately, and the group will then have fewer resources to complete their trip. Should anyone step on the floor instead of on one of the squares at any time, the group will receive a consequence—for example, going back to the starting point, having one or more group members lose the ability to speak or see (if the latter, use a clean blindfold), or losing a resource (square).

   In determining consequences, use your own judgment and let the activity's purpose guide you in your choices. For example, if you are trying to encourage leadership and vocal participation among shy and quiet group members, an effective consequence would be to take away the ability to speak from a few of the more vocal members.

4. Ask if there are any questions and answer them. However, do not offer information regarding possible consequences for stepping off a square. If asked, reply by saying something like "You never know what can happen."
5. Make sure everyone is behind the line of the starting point and that the next "station" or destination is well marked.
6. At this point, you can make up a story or scenario to make the activity even more interesting. For example, you could say that the group must go through a swamp and avoid the dangers there. Some rules must be observed: First, their feet must touch only the carpet squares as they move across the swamp. After all, swamps are homes to alligators, poisonous snakes, leeches, and so forth, so to step off the square can result in dire consequences. Second, they must demonstrate that they value their resources by maintaining physical contact with them at all times. In addition, they must always bring their resources (carpet squares) with them to the next station.

7. Have the group undertake their journey:
   - The group stands together at the starting point, holding their resources (carpet squares). Without stepping into the swamp, one of the group members tosses a carpet square onto the first station.
   - The entire group then moves onto the carpet square, bringing the remaining squares with them.
   - Once all of the group is on the first square at the first station, a group member tosses a carpet square onto the second station.
   - The group then moves together to the second station. Once at the second station, someone must retrieve the carpet square from the first station. (Typically, a group member reaches back to pick it up while other members provide support to prevent him from falling or stepping into the swamp, danger zone, etc.)
   - This process is repeated until the group reaches the end: "freedom."

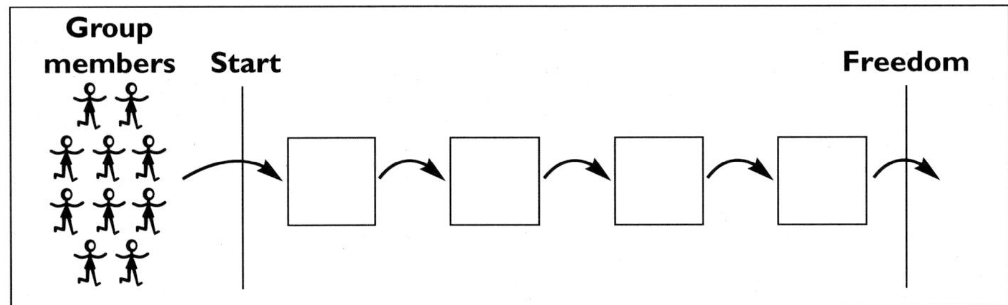

Processing the Activity

After the activity, reassemble the boys in the large group, and then process the experience. Focus on feelings, self-discovery, and levels of cooperation. Sample questions include the following:

- What was it like to work with people not in your *jamaa*?
- Who learned something about themselves? What was it?
- How did it feel when you first started out?
- (If consequences were given) What were you thinking and feeling when ____________________ happened?
- Why did/didn't you give up?

Ask the boys to relate the proverb and principle to the activity. Point out that our ancestors who braved the Underground Railroad faced beatings, branding, and even death if they were caught. It was only because they were brave, determined, cooperative, creative, and intelligent that many were able to escape to freedom.

---

6. Under the guidance of the *mzees*, students decide on a community project. Examples include:
   - Volunteering at a local food bank to help with the preparation and distribution of food.
   - Cleaning a local playground and if time permits, maintaining it.
   - Holding a car wash, with proceeds to be donated to their local senior or community center.
   - Cleaning or painting their Boys and Girls Club or other recreational facility.
   - Planning and carrying out a craft project in a senior citizen facility.

   The community activity should include a project that the boys can complete together. If possible, guide the boys to choose a place they can visit once the project is complete and reflect with pride upon what they have done.
7. Parents must be informed of the project and should be invited to participate. Permission for the boys' chosen project will have to be obtained from the proper authorities. Facilitators may have to be flexible with their schedules to accommodate the project.
8. Hand out the journals and pencils or pens, and give each boy a copy of the journal page for Session 7. Read through the journal page together and ask if there are any questions, then have the boys complete the page.
9. Collect the journals and distribute the *Staying in Focus* assignment cards for Session 7.

   "Do one positive thing for someone before the next session."

Read the assignment on the card and tell the boys that they should bring their cards to the next session and be ready to share their answers.

Closing Ritual

- Get the whole group's attention using the call and response method.
- Re-form the *durara umoja,* and have everyone read the *Brothers of Ujima Creed* together aloud.

Share the snacks. Mzees should use this opportunity to chat informally with all the boys. Encourage everyone to help with clean-up.

STAYING IN FOCUS ASSIGNMENT CARDS

Photocopy this page on card stock, then cut the cards apart (one card per participant).

SESSION 7: STAYING IN FOCUS

Do one positive thing for someone before the next session.

SESSION 7: STAYING IN FOCUS

Do one positive thing for someone before the next session.

SESSION 7: STAYING IN FOCUS

Do one positive thing for someone before the next session.

SESSION 7: STAYING IN FOCUS

Do one positive thing for someone before the next session.

SESSION 7: STAYING IN FOCUS

Do one positive thing for someone before the next session.

SESSION 7: STAYING IN FOCUS

Do one positive thing for someone before the next session.

SESSION 8

Creativity: Finding Your Talents

OBJECTIVES

- To help the boys develop greater appreciation for their talents
- To encourage boys to use creativity as a means of self expression and positive coping

MATERIALS

Music player and recorded African drumming or percussion music

Water and plant for the *tambiko*

Jamaas' rules posters

Books, videos, and prints from African American male authors and poets, playwrights, visual artists, and filmmakers

Easel pads and markers for each *jamaa*

Journals and copies of the Session 8 journal page (Appendix B, page 143)

Other materials depending upon planned creative activities (art supplies, musical instruments, etc.)

Staying in Focus assignment cards for Session 8 (page 84)

Snacks

PREPARATION

- Arrange participatory art and expressive activities (e.g., poetry jam, rapping, drumming, print making using Andinkra symbols, acting, etc.).
- Arrange for a guest speaker who is a local or regional creative artist. This could be a photographer, a painter, spoken word poet, singer, dancer, drummer, martial arts instructor, etc. (Carefully review your options to ensure that the content of the artist's work is consistent with the *Nguzo Nane*.)

PROCEDURE

Before the boys arrive, start the music. Continue to display the posters of the Nguzo Nane (Eight Principles) and Brothers of Ujima Creed, along with the map of Africa.

Opening Ritual

- Turn off the music. Gather everyone together for the *durara umoja*. *Mzees* should spread themselves throughout the circle.
- Perform the *tambiko*.

Instruct the boys to get out their Staying in Focus assignment cards and go to their jamaas.

Jamaa Work

1. Ask for three volunteers. Have one post the *jamaa's* rules poster and the other two write the *nguzo* and proverb of the day.

   Nguzo/Principle: Kuumba (Creativity)

   Proverb: "With your hands you make your success, with your hands you destroy your success."

2. Have all the students say the *nguzo*. Discuss the meaning of the proverb. Ask them to relate the proverb to the principle.

   Discussion Goals

   - Understanding the *nguzo* and proverb

- Understanding the value of creativity and the presence of creativity within African and African American cultures
- Supporting and clarifying individual and group opportunities to use creativity positively

Discussion Questions

- What does this proverb mean?
- What are some ways that people use their creativity and talents to build their community?
- What are some ways that some people use their creativity and talents to bring others down? Note that people can use their hands to be both creative and destructive.

3. Begin by discussing the last session's *Staying in Focus* assignment. Was there anyone you wanted to help but couldn't? Was there anyone you wanted to help, but who did not want your help?
4. Have the work of African American male writers, filmmakers, and artists stacked and displayed throughout the room. Ask the participants what these products and written work all have in common. Tell the boys that they were all created by African American men.
5. Ask the boys to name someone who they consider creative. Acknowledge their responses and make sure to mention that creativity comes in many forms. Acknowledge the creative work of African American men that may be outside of what is typically thought of as creative, such as being able to design a logo for a family website or Facebook page. Discuss the importance of creativity and share information on the creative achievements of African American males.
6. Assemble the boys into the larger group for the guest speaker's presentation. Let the boys know if the guest speaker comes from their community or a similar background
7. Have the boys participate in one of the following creative activities, or another activity under the supervision of the guest speaker.

Creative Activities

Activity Option I: Collage Posters: About Me

Materials and Supplies

Poster board of different colors

Markers

Colored paper

Scissors

Stickers and stamps (alphabet letters and positive images relevant to adolescent males)

Magazines with positive images

Other images, including photocopies of pictures from prior sessions and photographs brought in by the boys. If the program has a digital camera and printer, photos can be made on site.

> *Note: Take great care to protect important family photos. Use a copy machine to copy pictures or images the boys want to include in their collages. Store original photos carefully away from art materials so they will not be damaged.*

Have the boys use different materials to make a poster about themselves. Boys are encouraged to shape the poster around their interests, their goals, and their hopes. If smaller sizes of poster board are used and affordable frames available, these posters can be collected during this session and presented framed at the closing ceremony as a gift.

Activity Option II: Printing T-Shirts: About Me

Materials and Supplies

Cotton T-shirts (large or extra-large)

Fabric dye

Stamps with Adinkra symbols, or copies of Adinkra symbols and potatoes for making stamps. If you are making potato stamps, make sure the images are sized to fit on half of a potato cut cross- or length-wise.

Completed T-shirts as examples

- Session leaders present background on Adinkra symbols, and linkages to the history of the Ashanti people of Ghana. There are several websites about Adinkra symbols and their meanings, including http://www.adinkra.org/htmls/adinkra_index.htm
- Have the boys select symbols that represent themselves, then use stamps and fabric paint to stamp designs on T-shirts.
- Stamps can also be made from potatoes. First, cut a potato in half, crosswise or lengthwise depending on its size and shape. Then, place a reverse image of a symbol against the cut side and use a pencil point to transfer the outline of the image to the potato. Use a plastic knife to carefully cut away the "negative" portion of the image. Adults should assist with the cutting. Depending on the maturity of the group and the amount of time available for the session, you may choose to prepare potato stamps in advance.

---

8. Hand out the journals and pencils or pens, and give each boy a copy of the journal page for Session 8. Read through the journal page together and ask if there are any questions, then have the boys complete the page.
9. Distribute the *Staying in Focus* cards for Session 8.

   "Identify one way in which you express your creativity. Practice this before the next session."

   Read the assignment on the card and tell the boys that they should bring their cards to the next session and be ready to share their answers.

Closing Ritual

- Get the whole group's attention using the call and response method.
- Re-form the *durara umoja*, and have everyone read the *Brothers of Ujima Creed* together aloud.

  Share the snacks. Mzees use this opportunity to chat informally with all of the boys. Encourage everyone to help with clean-up.

STAYING IN FOCUS ASSIGNMENT CARDS

Photocopy this page on card stock, then cut the cards apart (one card per participant).

SESSION 8: STAYING IN FOCUS

Identify one way in which you express your creativity. Practice this before the next session.

SESSION 8: STAYING IN FOCUS

Identify one way in which you express your creativity. Practice this before the next session.

SESSION 8: STAYING IN FOCUS

Identify one way in which you express your creativity. Practice this before the next session.

SESSION 8: STAYING IN FOCUS

Identify one way in which you express your creativity. Practice this before the next session.

SESSION 8: STAYING IN FOCUS

Identify one way in which you express your creativity. Practice this before the next session.

SESSION 8: STAYING IN FOCUS

Identify one way in which you express your creativity. Practice this before the next session.

SESSION 9

Educational Awareness: Climbing the Ladder of Success

OBJECTIVES

- To explore and clarify the purpose of getting an education, cultivating knowledge, and expanding intellectual interest.
- To increase the boys' awareness of the long-term consequences of undervaluing education.
- To review and reflect on individual educational goals

MATERIALS

Music player and recorded African drumming or percussion music

Water and plant for the *tambiko*

Jamaas' rules posters

Journals and copies of the Session 9 journal page (Appendix B, page 144)

Pencils or pens

Easel pads and markers for each *jamaa*

Staying in Focus assignment cards for Session 9 (page 90)

Snacks

PREPARATION

- Identify and arrange for a panel of two or three speakers, including individuals with varying educational accomplishments. The speakers should be African American males. These may include a successful college student, an individual who is self-employed, and a professional (attorney, architect, college professor, engineer, etc.). Try to identify a speaker who is a model of educational success and who comes from a cultural or contextual background similar to that of the boys in the program.
- Prepare the speakers for the type of youth group, their expected participation and modeling in the *durara umoja*, the rationale and goals for the session, and what they are asked to contribute. Ask guest speakers to share with the boys their route to success and barriers they had to overcome. Suggested topics include overcoming obstacles, persistence and determination, decision making, responsibilities and leadership, community and family service, and setting goals as Black men. If they feel comfortable talking about bad choices and decisions they have made, encourage them to do so.
- (Optional) Assemble information on Historically Black Colleges and Universities (HBCUs). Information on HBCUs can be found on several internet sites, including: http://www.doi.gov/hrm/black.html
- If there is an HBCU within close proximity, facilitators can also provide basic information about the school (number of students, when it was formed, percentage of student body that is local, etc.). A student from this HBCU can be included on the panel of speakers.

PROCEDURE

Before the boys arrive, start the music. Continue to display the posters of the Nguzo Nane (Eight Principles) and Brothers of Ujima Creed, along with the map of Africa.

Opening Ritual

- Turn off the music. Gather everyone together for the *durara umoja*. *Mzees* should spread themselves throughout the circle. Ask the group to explain the significance of the *durara umoja*.

- Perform the *tambiko*.

Instruct the boys to get out their Staying in Focus assignment cards and go to their jamaas.

Jamaa Work

1. Ask for three volunteers. Have one post the *jamaa's* rules poster and the other two write the *nguzo* and proverb of the day.

   Nguzo/Principle: Nia (Purpose)

   Proverbs: "Knowledge is like a garden: if it is not cultivated, it cannot be harvested."

   "Lack of knowledge is darker than night."

2. Have all the students say the *nguzo*. Discuss the meaning of the proverb. Ask them to relate the proverb to the principle.

   Discussion Goals

   - Understanding the *nguzo* and proverb
   - Understanding the value of having a purpose
   - Supporting and clarifying individual and group opportunities to support positive outcomes obtained through purpose

   Discussion Questions

   - What does each proverb mean?
   - What does it mean to cultivate and harvest knowledge? Why is lacking knowledge described as being darker than night?
   - Remind the boys that education provides a way in which one's life purpose can be met.

3. Begin by discussing the previous session's *Staying in Focus* assignment. What did you create? Did you create something for someone else, such as a poem, a picture, or a song? Did your creation solve a problem or make something easier to do?

4. Hand out paper and pens or pencils, then ask the boys to write down what they would like to be when they grow older and why education is important to them.
5. Assemble the boys in the larger group for the speaker panel.
6. Introduce the speakers. Make sure to include in the introductory remarks any relevant connection of the speaker to the boys. This might include where they grew up, what their interests might have been as children and adolescents, etc.
7. Speakers address a topic related to goal obtainment, decision making, work environments, and the importance of education.
8. Once all speakers have finished, ask the boys to write down their goals once again and how they plan to obtain these goals.
9. The boys can then share their personal goals, and the speakers and *mzees* give feedback. Ask the boys what is one thing they can do before the next session to move them closer to their goal.
10. (Optional) Close the presentation with a discussion of historically Black institutions of higher learning and their importance.

Have the boys return to their jamaas.

11. Hand out the journals and pencils or pens, and give each boy a copy of the journal page for Session 9. Read through it with them and ask if they have any questions. Have the boys complete the page.
12. Distribute the *Staying in Focus* assignment cards for Session 9.

    "Write down one educational goal. Locate and identify one resource that can help support you in achieving that educational goal."

    Read the assignment on the card and tell the boys that they should bring their cards to the next session and be ready to share their answers.

Closing Ritual

- Get the whole group's attention using the call and response method.
- Re-form the *durara umoja*, and have everyone read the *Brothers of Ujima Creed* together aloud.

Share the snacks. Mzees use this opportunity to chat informally with all of the boys. Encourage everyone to help with clean-up.

STAYING IN FOCUS ASSIGNMENT CARDS

Photocopy this page on card stock, then cut the cards apart (one card per participant).

SESSION 9: STAYING IN FOCUS

Write down one educational goal.
Locate and identify one resource that can help support you in achieving that educational goal.

SESSION 9: STAYING IN FOCUS

Write down one educational goal.
Locate and identify one resource that can help support you in achieving that educational goal.

SESSION 9: STAYING IN FOCUS

Write down one educational goal.
Locate and identify one resource that can help support you in achieving that educational goal.

SESSION 9: STAYING IN FOCUS

Write down one educational goal.
Locate and identify one resource that can help support you in achieving that educational goal.

SESSION 9: STAYING IN FOCUS

Write down one educational goal.
Locate and identify one resource that can help support you in achieving that educational goal.

SESSION 9: STAYING IN FOCUS

Write down one educational goal.
Locate and identify one resource that can help support you in achieving that educational goal.

SESSION 10

Life Course

OBJECTIVES

- To help the boys gain an understanding of their talents, strengths, and assets in achieving their goals.
- To help boys see the connection between their life course and the talents and gifts they have.

MATERIALS

Music player and recorded African drumming or percussion music

Water and plant for the *tambiko*

Jamaas' rules posters

Journals and copies of the Session 10 journal page (Appendix B, page 145)

Pencils or pens

Easel pads and markers for each *jamaa*

Copies of life goal handouts (pages 96–101)

Staying in Focus assignment cards for Session 10 (page 102)

Snacks

PREPARATION

- Prepare index cards with several roles written on them, such as "student," "son," "grandson," "athlete," "leader," and others. Also have blank cards ready. Several different roles should be on each card rather than one specific role per card.

Make sure the number of cards prepared matches the number of boys. See the list below for different roles.

Roles		
Son	Student	Athlete
Brother	Neighbor	Friend
Nephew	Grandson	Cousin
Uncle	Employee	Boyfriend
Artist	Other: ____________________	

PROCEDURE

Before the boys arrive, start the music. Continue to display the posters of the Nguzo Nane (Eight Principles) and Brothers of Ujima Creed, along with the map of Africa.

Opening Ritual

- Turn off the music. Gather everyone together for the *durara umoja. Mzees* should spread themselves throughout the circle. Ask the group to explain the significance of the *durara umoja.* If no one responds, remind the students of its purpose and significance.
- Perform the *tambiko.*

Instruct the boys to get out their Staying in Focus assignment cards and go to their jamaas.

Jamaa Work

1. Once in their *jamaas,* students should turn their chairs so that they face the front of the room.
2. Have one of the senior *mzees* call the group to order and announce that the proverb and principle of the day will be discussed in the larger group. Select two students, one to write the *nguzo* (principle) and proverbs and another to read them aloud to the group.

Nguzo/Principle: Imani (Faith)

Proverbs: "Give a man a fish he will eat for a day; teach a man to fish he will eat for a lifetime."

"Be unable to handle an axe, but don't be unable to handle instruction."

3. All of the students repeat the *nguzo* and recite the proverbs together.

Discussion Goals

- Understanding the *nguzo* and proverb
- Understanding the value of faith
- Supporting and clarifying individual and group opportunities to support positive outcomes obtained through belief in self, belief in a higher power and belief in others.

At this point, mzees should be careful not to relate the nguzo (faith) to religion. In other words, stick to the idea of a higher spiritual belief without relating it to specific religious institutions.

Discussion Questions

- What do these proverbs mean? Can a person survive if they can't handle an ax? Can they survive if they can't take instruction?
- How do we see that people are given fish instead of being taught how to fish? Which do you want in your life?
- Why is faith important? Is faith just about what people believe in church or temple? What does it mean to have faith in oneself? What does it mean to have faith in others? What does it mean to have faith in ones people? How can faith be important to achieving one's goals?

4. Have students report on the *Staying in Focus* assignment from the previous session. Ask what they did to help them to reach their goals. Acknowledge the boys' answers but do not discuss them.
5. One of the senior *mzees* closes the discussion with a definition of faith. A sample definition is, "Faith is belief in yourself or something outside yourself. It means recognizing that you

can achieve by using your gifts and talents and working hard."

6. *Mzees* hand out journals and the journal page for Session 10. Do not discuss the entries.
7. Hand out "role" cards to the boys. Explain to the boys that each of them plays many roles in their community: student, son, grandson, athlete, and leader. Ask students if there are other roles that are important to them that are not listed on the cards, and offer them blank cards for any additional roles. Students then pick which roles are most important to them and which are least important. They are asked to indicate on their journal pages why some roles are important to them and why others are not.
8. Remind the boys that we have many gifts and talents, but that sometimes we hide those talents or do not let others see them. Ask the boys to list three gifts or talents that they possess that others know about, and one gift or talent that many people do not know about. Then, have them list two things at which they would like to be better. Finally, have them list three things they would like to accomplish (a) during their lifetimes; (b) in the next five years; and (c) in the next year. Have the boys describe what they are doing to achieve those things. Who are the people supporting them in achieving these goals, and what kind of support do they need?

   You may use the Goal Setting worksheets starting on page 96 to assist boys in generating goals across different areas, sorting them into long- and short-term goals. The boys can review their goals and work in a more targeted fashion on a specific set of short-term goals and related activities. There is also an Action Review worksheet on page 101 that can be used for documenting and reviewing goal-related action in later sessions.

9. Have the boys return to their *jamaas.* Focusing on the short-term activity sheet, the boys take turns serving in the role of "coach," giving feedback on the steps and strategies that other *jamaa* members have listed. Coaches can support their peers in practical goal achievement by asking questions such as, "Are there steps that are missing?" or "Are there other kinds of support that you might seek or other places or people

from whom you can obtain support?" The boys can provide feedback to one another on how helpful they were as coaches and how they can strengthen their supportive role for their brothers.

10. Discuss the concept of *persistence,* by asking the boys questions such as the following: Do people who achieve their goals give up? What about when you ask an adult for help or support and that person is too busy or says no—do you just give up? What are some options? When is it better to give up on that particular adult or resource and choose or identify another? What about when it is the adult's responsibility to provide support and he or she doesn't? Do you give up? What can you do?
11. Ask the boys to consider these questions: "Who is an adult you trust? Who is someone your age you trust?" Discuss the characteristics of someone who is trustworthy and someone who is not. Ask the boys, "What is it like to get feedback from someone who is not trustworthy?"
12. Collect the journals and pens or pencils, then distribute the *Staying in Focus* assignment cards for Session 10.

    "Ask two people (adults or peers) who know you, whom you trust, and who support you, to tell you two abilities or talents that they believe you have."

    Read the assignment on the card and tell the boys that they should bring their cards to the next session and be ready to share their answers.

Closing Ritual

- Get the whole group's attention using the call and response method.
- Re-form the *durara umoja,* and have everyone read the *Brothers of Ujima Creed* together aloud.

    Share the snacks. Mzees use this opportunity to chat informally with all of the boys. Encourage everyone to help with clean-up.

GOALS

Goals are specific things you want to accomplish in a certain period of time. There are many types of goals. For example, you might have a goal of saving a certain amount of money in a month. Or you may want to get a better grade in math. Other goals include making new friends, or learning to write music. The following list can give you an idea of the types of goal you can set for yourself. Look at the list and think about the goals you want to achieve. Then use the Individual Development Plans to help you figure out whether these goals are short-term or long-term and what you have to learn or do to accomplish them.

Family Goals

Financial Goals

Career Goals

Spiritual Goals

Physical and Health Goals

Social Goals

Educational Goals

Recreational Goals

Lifestyle Goals

Creative Goals

Ability (Learning) Goals

"Giving" and Sharing Goals

Achievement Goals

My Other Goals

INDIVIDUAL DEVELOPMENT PLAN (LIFE-LONG)

Name Date

Goal to Be Achieved	My Values (Why is this important to me?)	My Abilities and Interests	Resources and Supports Needed or Helpful (money, time, etc.)	Barriers and Challenges	Actions to Be Taken
Life-long					
Long-range (in the next 5 years)					
Mid-term (in the next year)					
Short-term (in the next 3 months)					

INDIVIDUAL DEVELOPMENT PLAN (SHORT-TERM)

Name Date

Goal to Be Achieved	**Resources and Supports Needed or Helpful** (money, time, etc.)	**Barriers and Challenges**	**Actions to Be Taken**	**Priorities** (What do I need to do first? And then next? And then? And then . . .?)
Short-term (in the next 3 months)				

ASSESSMENT OF MY GOALS

Goal	Is this a good goal for me?	How realistic is my goal	Can I make my goal clearer?	How much is my goal under my control	How much am I willing to invest in this goal to achieve it?
Family					
Career					
Spiritual					
Physical and Health					
Social					
Educational					
Recreational					
Creative					
Giving and Sharing					
Other					

STRENGTHS, TALENTS, AND ABILITIES

What are my strengths, talents and abilities?

What do I think I need to work on?

What would my best friend say are my strengths and talents?

What would my best friend say I need to work on?

Think of an adult who knows you well and cares for you.

What might this person say are my strengths and talents?

What might this person say I need to work on?

GOAL ACTION REVIEW WORKSHEET

Name:

Goal:

What's the next step will I take to achieve my goal?

When will I accomplish this?

Date:

What action did I actually take?

How did it work out?

What do I need to do next?

Signature/Date

STAYING IN FOCUS ASSIGNMENT CARDS

Photocopy this page on card stock, then cut the cards apart (one card per participant).

SESSION 10: STAYING IN FOCUS

Ask two people (adults or peers) who know you, whom you trust, and who support you, to tell you two abilities or talents that they believe you have.

SESSION 10: STAYING IN FOCUS

Ask two people (adults or peers) who know you, whom you trust, and who support you, to tell you two abilities or talents that they believe you have.

SESSION 10: STAYING IN FOCUS

Ask two people (adults or peers) who know you, whom you trust, and who support you, to tell you two abilities or talents that they believe you have.

SESSION 10: STAYING IN FOCUS

Ask two people (adults or peers) who know you, whom you trust, and who support you, to tell you two abilities or talents that they believe you have.

SESSION 10: STAYING IN FOCUS

Ask two people (adults or peers) who know you, whom you trust, and who support you, to tell you two abilities or talents that they believe you have.

SESSION 10: STAYING IN FOCUS

Ask two people (adults or peers) who know you, whom you trust, and who support you, to tell you two abilities or talents that they believe you have.

SESSION 11

Choices and Challenges

OBJECTIVES

- To develop a collective and personal working definition for coping
- To help boys develop new and positive ways of coping

MATERIALS

Music player and recorded African drumming or percussion music

Water and plant for the *tambiko*

Jamaas' rules posters

Journals and copies of the Session 11 journal page (Appendix A, page 146)

Pencils or pens

Easel pads and markers for each *jamaa*

Copies of handouts on *Statistics on African American Males* and *Cultural Forms of Coping* (pages 107–108)

Staying in Focus assignment cards for Session 11 (page 109)

Snacks

PREPARATION

- Review handout on cultural forms of coping:
  - Social Support and Communalism
  - Spirituality and Use of Ritual
  - Cognitive and Emotional Coping Strategies

PROCEDURE

Before the boys arrive, start the music. Continue to display the posters of the Nguzo Nane (Eight Principles) and Brothers of Ujima Creed, along with the map of Africa.

Opening Ritual

- Turn off the music. Gather everyone together for the *durara umoja*. *Mzees* should spread themselves throughout the circle.
- Perform the *tambiko*.

Instruct the boys to get out their Staying in Focus assignment cards and go to their jamaas.

Jamaa Work

1. Ask for three volunteers. Have one post the *jamaa's* rules poster and the other two write the *nguzo* and proverb of the day.

   Nguzo/Principle: Kujichagulia (Self-Determination)

   Proverb: "The beak of the bird is what tells us the things it eats."

2. Have all the students say the *nguzo*. Discuss the meaning of the proverb. Ask them to relate the proverb to the principle.

   Discussion Goals

   - Understanding the *nguzo* and proverb
   - Understanding the value of self-determination
   - Supporting and clarifying individual and group behavioral choices and their linkage to directing one's own path. This is in contrast to making choices that result in others taking away choices and autonomy.

   Discussion Questions

   - What does this proverb mean?
   - What different kinds of birds have different kinds of beaks? Why do they have these different beaks? What are different kinds of beaks good for? What about people?

- Can we judge a book by its cover?
- How does what we see of a person help us understand them? Can behavior be a sort of beak?

3. Begin by discussing the last session's *Staying in Focus* assignment.
4. This session's *jamaa* work will continue with a discussion of the following statistics. A sample introduction might be, "There is no way one can address the problems facing African American boys and men until they know what those problems are. Here are some statistics about African American males today."
5. Ask the boys, "How do you feel when you hear this?" Do you think these statistics are true? Discuss whether or not they know African American men and boys who fit these statistics. Students most likely will be familiar with boys and men who fit these statistics, but also ask them if they know people who do not fit these statistics.
6. Following the discussion, the *mzee* explains that the group will move toward developing coping techniques. Ask the boys to collectively develop a working definition for "coping."
7. Have the boys generate a list of challenges that are specific to African American men and youth. These may include challenges in economic circumstances and family and social relationships.
8. *Jamaas* work together to identify effective solutions to these challenges. Why are they effective?
9. To get the boys thinking about coping strategies and solving problems, you might ask the boys to think of a successful African American man and think about how he would act if confronted with a problem. How would he cope with the situation? If the boys do not have specific ideas, discuss with them some positive ways to cope that fit within African American culture. Some of these are included on the *Cultural Forms of Coping* handout.
10. Hand out the journals and pencils or pens, and give each boy a copy of the journal page for Session 11. Read through it with them and ask if they have any questions. Have the boys complete the page.

11. Distribute the *Staying in Focus* assignment cards for Session 11.

    "Share one new thing you've learned with someone not in the *Brothers of Ujima* program."

    Read the assignment on the card and tell the boys that they should bring their cards to the next session and be ready to share their answers.

Closing Ritual

- Get the whole group's attention using the call and response method.
- Re-form the *durara umoja*, and have everyone read the *Brothers of Ujima Creed* together aloud.

    Share the snacks. Mzees use this opportunity to chat informally with all of the boys. Encourage everyone to help with clean-up.

STATISTICS ABOUT AFRICAN AMERICAN MALES

- There are 1.03 Black boys born in the United States for every 1.00 Black girls.
- Seventy percent of all African American male children are born into single-parent (female) headed households.
- The 4-year high school graduation rate for African American males is only 47 percent.
- Black boys make up 20 percent of the children who are labeled by the schools as mentally disabled.
- African-American boys represent 37 percent of school suspensions.
- Black men make up only 5 percent of college students in the United States.
- One in 5 black males without a high school diploma is incarcerated.
- One out of 4 black males aged 20 to 29 is either in prison, on parole, or on probation
- Forty-four percent of state and federal prisoners are African Americans.
- African American men have the lowest life expectancy of any racial or gender group.
- African American men have the highest homicide rate of any group.
- African American men have the highest cancer rate of any group.
- As of May 2011, 1 in 6 African American men over the age of 20 was unemployed.
- As of May 2011, 2 in 5 African American teens were unemployed.
- About 1 in 3 African American male children lives in poverty.

Sources: U.S. Department of Education, National Center for Education Statistics (2000; 2010); U.S. Census Bureau (2010), American Community Survey Reports: The Black Community 2004.

CULTURAL FORMS OF COPING

Social Support and Communalism

- Talking to friends about your problems
- Asking parents and family to help you identify solutions to your problems
- Asking for help from a teacher or older adult
- Talking to a person whom you admire and respect

Spirituality and Use of Ritual

- Praying or reading an inspirational message
- Talking to a religious or spiritual leader
- When stressed, repeating a behavior that helps to calm you down, such as lighting a candle or meditating

Cognitive and Emotional Coping

- Planning how you can change things
- Writing down what is wrong and what steps you can take to change things
- Learning to identify what creates stress in your life
- Doing positive things that make you feel better, such as running, playing a game of basketball, taking a walk, or another form of physical activity
- Thinking about your ancestors and what they had to endure to survive

Reference: Utsey, S., Adams, E., & Bolden, M. (2000). Development and initial validation of the Africultural Coping Systems Inventory. *Journal of Black Psychology*, 26(2), 194-215.

STAYING IN FOCUS ASSIGNMENT CARDS

Photocopy this page on card stock, then cut the cards apart (one card per participant).

SESSION 11: STAYING IN FOCUS

Share one new thing you've learned with someone not in the *Brothers of Ujima* program.

SESSION 11: STAYING IN FOCUS

Share one new thing you've learned with someone not in the *Brothers of Ujima* program.

SESSION 11: STAYING IN FOCUS

Share one new thing you've learned with someone not in the *Brothers of Ujima* program.

SESSION 11: STAYING IN FOCUS

Share one new thing you've learned with someone not in the *Brothers of Ujima* program.

SESSION 11: STAYING IN FOCUS

Share one new thing you've learned with someone not in the *Brothers of Ujima* program.

SESSION 11: STAYING IN FOCUS

Share one new thing you've learned with someone not in the *Brothers of Ujima* program.

SESSION 12

How Do I Work It Out?

OBJECTIVES

- To develop collective and personal strategies for dealing with conflict
- To help boys develop new and positive ways of conflict management

MATERIALS

Music player and recorded African drumming or percussion music

Water and plant for the *tambiko*

Jamaas' rules posters

Journals and copies of the Session 12 journal page (Appendix A, page 147)

Pencils or pens

Easel pads and markers for each *jamaa*

Copies of handout on *Challenging Life Situations* (pages 115–116)

TV and VCR/DVD or computer with video capability

Staying in Focus assignment cards for Session 12 (page 118)

Snacks

PREPARATION

- Compose an invitation to the closing ceremony to be mailed to guests who will be identified by the boys at the end of this session. A sample invitation appears on page 117.

- Identify and secure appropriate video clips illustrating conflict and its resolution. They can be found on YouTube or VHS/DVD; some suggestions appear below.

Video Resources

Stomp the Yard **(PG-13) Sony Pictures (2007)**

- Themes: Conflict resolution, betrayal/revenge, old versus new, group versus individual priorities
- DVD Scene 19–end of movie

This clip includes references to the impact of past behavior upon the lives of youth, especially youth from communities that are saturated with a wide range of criminal influences. These scenes also demonstrate how culturally salient activities, in this case stepping and urban dance, can create bonds of healthy peer-to-peer relationships and high levels of belonging and social bonding.

You Got Served **(PG-13) Sony Pictures (2004)**

- Themes: Conflict resolution, poor judgment, and criminal influences
- DVD Scenes 12, 13, 16, 19, 24

This series of scenes captures several challenges and conflicts caused by confused priorities and poor judgment. It emphasizes the importance of peer relationships and influences upon youth. These scenes also suggest the proximal influences of criminal elements within the lives of urban African American youth. It covers the temptation to access illegal financial resources when legitimate financial resources may be inaccessible or unavailable.

PROCEDURE

Before the boys arrive, start the music. Continue to display the posters of the Nguzo Nane (Eight Principles) and Brothers of Ujima Creed, along with the map of Africa.

Opening Ritual

- Turn off the music. Gather everyone together for the *durara umoja*. *Mzees* should spread themselves throughout the circle.

- Perform the *tambiko*.

    Instruct the boys to get out their Staying in Focus assignment cards and go to their jamaas.

Jamaa Work

1. Ask for three volunteers. Have one post the *jamaa's* rules poster and the other two write the *nguzo* and proverb of the day.

    Nguzo/Principle: Heshema (Respect)

    Proverb: "It is better to be loved than feared."

2. Have all the students say the *nguzo*. Discuss the meaning of the proverb. Ask them to relate the proverb to the principle.

    Discussion Goals

    - Understanding the *nguzo* and proverb
    - Understanding the value of respect
    - Supporting and clarifying how we give and receive respect

    Discussion Questions

    - What does this proverb mean?
    - What are the plusses and minuses of being feared? What are the plusses and minuses of being loved?
    - What do you want in your lives?
    - What does fear mean for an individual? For a family? For a community?
    - What does love mean for an individual? For a family? For a community?

3. Have two or three boys report on the *Staying in Focus* assignment for the previous session.
4. Reassemble in the larger group. Show the selected video clips, then facilitate a 5- to 10-minute discussion. Ask the boys to comment on the video clip. How do they think the characters felt? How could they have handled the situation differently? Identify a character and ask the boys what they would say to him.
5. Using the *Challenging Life Situations* handout, have the boys perform role plays demonstrating proper and improper ways

of handling conflicts. Each *jamaa* will perform a skit for the larger group (about 3 to 4 minutes).

6. Have the boys return to their *jamaas.* Hand out the journals and pencils or pens, and give each boy a copy of the journal page for Session 12. Read through it with them and ask if they have any questions. Have the boys complete the page.
7. Collect the journals and pens or pencils, then distribute the *Staying in Focus* assignment cards for Session 12.

   "Identify one difficult situation you have faced. Consider how well you handled the situation. Is there anything you could have done to handle it better?"

   Read the assignment on the card and tell the boys that they should bring their cards to the next session and be ready to share their answers.

Closing Ceremony Announcement

- Inform the boys that there are two sessions left in the program and that the last session will include a closing ceremony. Provide an overview of what the event will entail. Discuss assignments for the event (e.g., *jamaas* will present each of the *Nguzo Nane*, its definition, a relevant proverb and why this is important to the African American community). Let the boys know that they will work on these presentations in the next session.
- Generate a list of guests (friends, family, and community elders). Prepare and send invitations for the closing ceremony to be held at the last session. A sample invitation appears on page 117.

Closing Ritual

- Get the whole group's attention using the call and response method.
- Re-form the *durara umoja*, and have everyone read the *Brothers of Ujima Creed* together aloud.

  Share the snacks. Mzees use this opportunity to chat informally with all of the boys. Encourage everyone to help with clean-up.

CHALLENGING LIFE SITUATIONS

Situation 1

A group of friends tells Trey that another student in the school, Tyrone, has been trying to talk to Trey's girlfriend, Alicia. Trey runs into Tyrone after school.

Characters: Trey, Tyrone, a group of friends.

Situation 2

Alex is a really good student but he's pretty low key and quiet about his school work. In class, his teacher announces that Alex has made the highest score on the math test. Another classmate, Ricardo, loudly comments, "That ain't nothing!"

Characters: Alex, teacher, Ricardo, classmates.

Situation 3

Anthony hears that D'Antonio is planning to fight Anthony on his way home after school today. Anthony is on his way home and turns around to see D'Antonio and his friends walking behind him.

Characters: Anthony, D'Antonio, friends of the two boys.

Situation 4

Jamal's friends are planning to hang out together after school, but Jamal's mother says that he has to stay in and help take care of his little brother and sister. Jamal's friends press him to join them and call him "Momma's boy."

Characters: Jamal, Jamal's mother, Jamal's friends.

Situation 5

D'Andre forgets to bring in his homework today; in front of the class, his teacher says, "This is why Black men don't amount to anything."

Characters: D'Andre, classmates, teacher.

Situation 6

Ahmed's family is poor and he rarely wears clothing that is in fashion. After class, Ramel starts teasing Ahmed about his clothes and shoes.

Characters: Ahmed, Ramel, classmates.

Situation 7

In the last game of the season, rather than passing the ball to his teammate Jonathan, who is clearly open with an easy shot, Jason tries and misses an almost impossible shot.

Characters: Jason, Jonathan, teammates.

Situation 8

Eric puts his iPod in his locker but it is gone after gym class. He sees another classmate, Raymond—who has never brought an iPod to school—with an iPod identical to the one Eric can't find.

Characters: Eric, Raymond, classmates.

SAMPLE LETTER TO PARENTS AND GUARDIANS

[Your letterhead]

Date ________________

Dear Parents and Guardians:

Please join us in recognizing your son for his accomplishments in completing the *Brothers of Ujima* program. An awards ceremony will take place on _________ [date/time] at the following location:

____

____

All family members are invited, and refreshments will be served following the recognition ceremony.

Please RSVP no later than __________ [date] by calling ________________ .

Sincerely,

Program Coordinator

STAYING IN FOCUS ASSIGNMENT CARDS

Photocopy this page on card stock, then cut the cards apart (one card per participant).

SESSION 12: STAYING IN FOCUS

Identify one difficult situation you have faced. Consider how well you handled the situation. Is there anything you could have done to handle it better?

SESSION 12: STAYING IN FOCUS

Identify one difficult situation you have faced. Consider how well you handled the situation. Is there anything you could have done to handle it better?

SESSION 12: STAYING IN FOCUS

Identify one difficult situation you have faced. Consider how well you handled the situation. Is there anything you could have done to handle it better?

SESSION 12: STAYING IN FOCUS

Identify one difficult situation you have faced. Consider how well you handled the situation. Is there anything you could have done to handle it better?

SESSION 12: STAYING IN FOCUS

Identify one difficult situation you have faced. Consider how well you handled the situation. Is there anything you could have done to handle it better?

SESSION 12: STAYING IN FOCUS

Identify one difficult situation you have faced. Consider how well you handled the situation. Is there anything you could have done to handle it better?

SESSION 13

African American Male Leadership

OBJECTIVES

- To help participants understand the importance of leadership in their families, their communities, and their personal lives.
- To help boys learn to identify leadership qualities and distinguish the difference between leaders and dominant, selfish people
- To provide examples of dynamic and positive African and African American male leaders

MATERIALS

Music player and recorded African drumming or percussion music

Water and plant for the *tambiko*

Jamaas' rules posters

TV and VCR/DVD or computer with internet capability

Journals and copies of the Session 13 journal page (Appendix A, page 148)

Pencils or pens

Easel pads and markers for each *jamaa*

Staying in Focus assignment cards for Session 13 (page 124)

Snacks

PREPARATION

- Select a video clip from the MTV program *Making the Band* (available on DVD or on mtv.com). Another possible clip can come from the movie *Boys 'N the Hood,* available on DVD. Be sure to review clips for appropriateness given the ages of participants and the local norms.
- Identify local, national, and international examples of Black male leaders. Prepare information sheets with pictures of these leaders and brief descriptions of their achievements.
- Print the eight *nguzos* on separate sheets or cards to be assigned to groups for their closing ceremony presentations.

PROCEDURE

Before the boys arrive, start the music. Continue to display the posters of the Nguzo Nane (Eight Principles) and Brothers of Ujima Creed, along with the map of Africa.

Opening Ritual

- Turn off the music. Gather everyone together for the *durara umoja. Mzees* should spread themselves throughout the circle.
- Perform the *tambiko.*

Instruct the boys to get out their Staying in Focus assignment cards and go to their jamaas.

Jamaa Work

1. Ask for three volunteers. Have one post the *jamaa's* rules poster and the other two write the *nguzo* and proverb of the day.

   Nguzo/Principle: Ujima (Collective Work and Responsibility)

   Proverb: "Lead by example."
2. Have all the students say the *nguzo.* Discuss the meaning of the proverb. Ask them to relate the proverb to the principle.

Discussion Goals

- Understanding the *nguzo* and proverb
- Understanding the value of leadership
- Supporting and clarifying individual and group opportunities to support positive outcomes obtained through leadership

Discussion Questions

- What does this proverb mean?
- Who are some individuals you think are great leaders? What do you think made them good leaders?
- Have you heard someone say, "Don't do what I do, do what I say?" Does that work for a good leader? Why or why not?
- What happens when people find out a leader is a bad example? How can leaders hurt the people that follow them? Should you follow a leader even when you know he is wrong?

3. Begin the session by discussing the last session's *Staying in Focus* assignment.
4. Play an excerpt from the MTV television show *Making the Band*, which shows how Sean Combs provided leadership for the new group he had put together. He also spoke of the responsibilities of being a leader. You may also select and show a contemporary clip from a television, film, or other media source. The clip should convey positive leadership from an African American man.
5. (Optional) Have the boys use the internet, books, or other resources to search for and identify African American male leaders from local, national, and international media. Make sure that specific leaders reflect the cultural values congruent with the program.
6. On the easel pad, write: "Why is leadership important?" Prompt the boys to think in terms of what leaders do in teams, groups, families, and communities. For example, leaders stand up for the values of their group. They also are "examples" of how everyone should act and speak. They are the first to call for change in their communities, but they also provide

encouragement and support when things are going well. One definition might be: "True leadership is the encouragement and uplifting of others. It is teaching and sharing knowledge for the improvement and greater well-being of your family, friends, and community."

7. Ask the group to identify leaders in their families and communities. Share the information sheets on local, national, and international Black male leaders. Facilitators should cite individuals who demonstrate both aspects of leadership: (1) they stand up for what's right or best for the group, and (2) they are walking and talking examples of the values they stand up for. The boys should understand that bullies aren't leaders because bullies act in their own interest, not in the best interest of the group. Someone who gets people to do what he or she wants through intimidation is not a leader. While there may be times when a leader must be very firm to get the group or team to do what needs to be done, a true leader will treat people with respect even while being assertive. Facilitators should try to get the boys to think of hypothetical examples of leaders, in addition to actual individuals. A leader could be the father who sets an example of how he expects his children to act, while at the same time doing what's best for the family. A leader could also be the friend who stands up for what is right, even when it means risking ridicule or even physical harm.
8. Inform the boys that the next activity will require them to work together as a group in ways that will allow each of them, in their own way, to be a leader. Reinforce the point that a leader basically does two things. First, they speak and act in the best interest of their group, treating everyone with respect and providing encouragement. Second, leaders act the way they want others to act, by treating everyone they way they want to be treated. Reinforce the concepts that leaders put group interest ahead of self interest, and that someone who uses intimidation to put self interest ahead of group interest is a bully.
9. Group Activity: *Jamaas* prepare their presentations of their selected *nguzo* or *nguzos* (depending on the number of groups). *Nguzos* are assigned to *jamaas* so that all eight are presented. Groups may use their creativity to present the *nguzo*, its meaning, and a relevant proverb, and indicate why

this is important in the community. After the group work, each *jamaa* should discuss leadership. How did leadership play a role in their decision making and in their work. What worked? What did not?

10. Hand out the journals and pencils or pens, and give each boy a copy of the journal page for Session 13. Read through it with them and ask if they have any questions. Have the boys complete the page.
11. Collect the journals and pens or pencils, then distribute the *Staying in Focus* assignment cards for Session 13.

    "Identify two African American leaders you admire. Describe what it is that you admire about them."

    Read the assignment on the card and tell the boys that they should bring their cards to the next session and be ready to share their answers.

Closing Ritual

- Get the whole group's attention using the call and response method.
- Re-form the *durara umoja*, and have everyone read the *Brothers of Ujima Creed* together aloud.
- Remind the boys that the next session will be final one.
- Remind them of their roles in the closing ceremony. Request that the boys dress to show respect for this event—this may mean different things for different youth. Diversity should be respected.
- Ask for a volunteer to explain and perform the *tambiko* at the closing ceremony.
- (Optional) Ask for a volunteer to make a presentation on the topic "What *Brothers of Ujima* Means to Me" at the closing ceremony.
- (Optional) Invite community leaders and others community members who are interested in and/or who have supported program.

Share the snacks. Mzees use this opportunity to chat informally with all of the boys. Encourage everyone to help with clean-up.

STAYING IN FOCUS ASSIGNMENT CARDS

Photocopy this page on card stock, then cut the cards apart (one card per participant).

SESSION 13: STAYING IN FOCUS

Identify two African American leaders you admire. Describe what it is that you admire about them.

SESSION 13: STAYING IN FOCUS

Identify two African American leaders you admire. Describe what it is that you admire about them.

SESSION 13: STAYING IN FOCUS

Identify two African American leaders you admire. Describe what it is that you admire about them.

SESSION 13: STAYING IN FOCUS

Identify two African American leaders you admire. Describe what it is that you admire about them.

SESSION 13: STAYING IN FOCUS

Identify two African American leaders you admire. Describe what it is that you admire about them.

SESSION 13: STAYING IN FOCUS

Identify two African American leaders you admire. Describe what it is that you admire about them.

SESSION 14

Graduation and Closing Ceremony

OBJECTIVES

- To assist participants in gaining a new appreciation of their development and roles as members of the African American community
- To close out the program with a graduation ceremony

MATERIALS

Music player and recorded African drumming or percussion music

Water and plant for the *tambiko*

Pencils or pens

Copies of the Certificate of Recognition for all participants (page 128)

PREPARATION

- Prepare and send invitations to parents, family and community members at least two weeks in advance
- Make arrangements for special snacks or meal for participants and invited guests
- Make or purchase a small gift for each participant, such as a kente cloth stole or a book. All the gifts should be identical.
- (Optional) Arrange for a special cultural performance, such as African drumming, stepping, or dance.

PROCEDURE

Before the boys and guests arrive, start the music. Continue to display the posters of the Nguzo Nane (Eight Principles) and Brothers of Ujima Creed, along with the map of Africa.

Opening Ritual

- Turn off the music. Gather everyone together for the *durara umoja*. *Mzees* should spread themselves throughout the circle.
- A senior *mzee* announces that the closing ceremony will now begin. Have the boy who volunteered at the last session explain and perform the *tambiko*.

Instruct the boys to get out their Staying in Focus assignment cards and go to their jamaas.

Jamaa Work

1. Discuss the *Staying in Focus* assignment from the last session. Who are the leaders of your family and community? What makes them good leaders? What qualities do they have that you would like to have?
2. The students should turn their chairs so that they face the front of the room. One of the senior *mzees* calls the group to order. Selected students (making sure each *jamaa* is represented) will present each of the *Nguzo Nane*, its meaning, a relevant proverb, and why it is important to the community.
3. (Optional) Have a volunteer make a presentation on the topic "What *Brothers of Ujima* Means to Me."
4. Share the meal or snacks, and hold the cultural performance. If possible, have the boys participate in the performance.
5. (Optional) A representative from the boys' community service site comes to describe the service project and to thank the boys for their service and contributions to the community.

Closing Ceremony

1. Have an *mzee* or program person begin with brief remarks of his choice. Include a thank-you to the parents and community leaders for the opportunity to work with the boys as part of their movement toward manhood. The *mzee* may also indicate

that the program has stressed the responsibility that African American boys have to each other.

2. Have all the *mzees* and the boys stand. One mzee will speak to the boys and say:
   - You are all important members of the African American community.
   - You have many gifts to offer those around you.
   - We are excited and hopeful for who you will become.
   - We are already very blessed by who you are.
   - "From those to whom much is given, much is expected."
   - We have high expectations for each and every one of you.
3. An *mzee* from each *jamaa* will then come to the front with the certificates. The other *mzees* remain with the *jamaas* to distribute the gifts.
4. Have a senior *mzee* say, "These gifts symbolize how far you've come on your journey as a *Brother of Ujima*."
5. *Mzees* take turns calling individual *jamaa* members up front to receive their certificates. As each boy comes to the front, an *mzee* greets the boy with "Welcome, brother. You have come a long way." When the boy returns to his *jamaa*, another *mzee* presents him with a small gift.

Closing Ritual

If you wish, you can have parents and other invited guests participate in the durara umoja.

- After the certificates and gifts have been presented, call the group to order using the call and response method, and form the *durara umoja*.
- At this point, *mzees* from each *jamaa* may briefly identify a "gift" they have received from the boys. It may be something they learned or perhaps a new experience or insight.
- Close by encouraging the boys to continue to remember and practice what they've learned and by reciting the *Brother of Ujima Creed* together.

Mzees chat informally with the boys and their parents or caregivers. Participants help with clean-up.

CERTIFICATE OF ACHIEVEMENT

This certifies that

____

is awarded special recognition for his commitment
to cultural enrichment and participation in

BROTHERS OF UJIMA

Given at ______________________ this _____ day of ____________

______________________ Program Coordinator

______________________ *Mzee*

OPTIONAL SESSION

Kwanzaa

OBJECTIVES

- To familiarize boys with a cultural celebration of African Americans
- To provide the boys with an opportunity to participate in a Kwaanza celebration

MATERIALS

Music player and recorded African drumming or percussion music

Water and plant for the *tambiko*

Copies of the Kwanzaa handout (page 132)

Craft materials for the gift-making activity (jewelry, soaps, etc.)

Snacks

PREPARATION

- Obtain and arrange the following Kwanzaa symbols and decorations:

  Mkeka—a straw mat at least 2 x 3 feet

  Kinara—a candle holder that will hold seven candles

  Mishumaa Saba—three red, one black, and three green candles for the *Kinara*

  Muhindi—ears of dried corn

  Kikombe cha Umoja—a cup or goblet (Unity Cup)

  Mazao—a basket of fruits and vegetables

- Place the *mkeka* on a low table or the floor. Additional decorations may include Kente cloth, mud cloth, and other fabrics of African design; books about Kwanzaa; African art; and so forth.

PROCEDURE

Before the boys arrive, start the music. Continue to display the posters of the Nguzo Nane (Eight Principles) and Brothers of Ujima Creed, along with the map of Africa.

Opening Ritual

- Turn off the music. Gather everyone together for the *durara umoja*. *Mzees* should spread themselves throughout the circle.
- Perform the *tambiko*.

Group Discussion

1. Introduce Kwanzaa by asking the boys if any of them have attended a Kwanzaa celebration and/or can tell the group what it is. If no one responds, ask them to guess or tell what they think it is.
2. If you wish, distribute copies of the Kwanzaa handout. Explain the history and symbolism of Kwanzaa. It is important that the boys understand that it is not a religious observance and does not replace Christmas or other religious holidays for those who observe it.
3. Lead the group through the lighting of all of the *Mishumaa Saba* (candles). Boys from each *jamaa* may be called to light a candle.

Gift Making

1. Have the boys go to their *jamaas*. Tell the boys, if they don't already know, that one of the traditions of Kwanzaa is making gifts to give to others.
2. Pass out the craft supplies and have the boys make the gifts.

Closing Ritual

- Get the whole group's attention using the call and response method.
- Re-form the *durara umoja*, and have everyone read the *Brothers of Ujima Creed* together aloud.

Share the snacks. Mzees chat informally with all of the boys. Encourage everyone to help with clean-up.

KWANZAA

Kwanzaa is an African and African American holiday, celebrated from December 26 through January 1, that celebrates family, community and culture. It was created in 1966 by Dr. Maulana Karenga, a professor in the Department of Black Studies at California State University in Long Beach, California. The rituals of Kwanzaa are rooted in the first harvest celebrations of Africa. Kwanzaa is a cultural holiday, not a religious one, and is therefore available to and practiced by Africans and African Americans of all religious faiths.

KWANZAA SYMBOLS AND THEIR MEANINGS

Mazao (the crops)
African harvest and the rewards of productive and collective labor

Mkeka (the mat)
Tradition, history, and the foundation on which to build

Kinara (the candle holder)
African roots, our ancestors from Africa

Muhindi (the corn)
Children and our future

Mishumaa Saba (the Seven Candles)
Representing the Nguzo Saba, the Seven Principles that African and African American people are urged to live by

Kikombe cha Umoja (the Unity Cup)
The principle and practice of unity, which make all else possible

Zawadi (gifts)
The labor and love of parents and the commitments made and kept by children

APPENDIX A

Brothers of Ujima Journal

BROTHERS OF UJIMA JOURNAL

My Name

____

My *Jamaa* Name

____

The Meaning of My *Jamaa* Name

____

My *Mzee*'s Name

____

Date

____

BROTHERS OF UJIMA CREED

- We will learn about and trust our talents and abilities.
- We accept responsibility for what we do, who we are, and what we can become.
- We will work to help each other by acknowledging and supporting the talents and gifts within our brothers, within ourselves, and within our community.
- We will not act negatively toward or belittle our brothers, our sisters, or our community.
- We will show respect to our brothers, to ourselves, and to our community.

SESSION 2: NIA (PURPOSE)

A paddle here, a paddle there, the canoe stands still.

1. **Write the names of the members of your *jamaa*.**

2. **What does the name of your *jamaa* mean?**

3. **Write down two things you can contribute to your *jamaa*.**

SESSION 3: KUJICHAGULIA (SELF-DETERMINATION)

Disease and disasters come and go like rain,
but health is like the sun that illuminates the entire village.

1. **What is one thing I can do for good nutrition?**

2. **Why are sleep and rest important?**

3. **What can I do to be fit?**

4. **Name a behavior that can put my health at risk. What can I do to avoid that risk?**

5. **What is one way to show good sportsmanship?**

6. **Why is it important to be a good sport?**

SESSION 4: UMOJA (UNITY)

When elephants jostle, what gets hurt is the grass.

1. **Why is teamwork important?**

2. **What are helpful ways to provide support?**

3. **What are unhelpful ways to provide support?**

4. **What does it mean to be a positive Black man?**

5. **What does it mean to be a *Brother of Ujima*?**

SESSION 5: UMOJA (UNITY)

The ruin of a nation begins in the homes of its people.

What do you think about Africa?

1. **Africa is . . .**

2. **African people are . . .**

3. **When I hear the word "Africa," I think . . .**

4. **Africans probably think America is / Americans are . . .**

5. **Some things I would like to know about Africa are . . .**

6. **I would (or would not) like to visit Africa because . . .**

SESSION 6: UMOJA (UNITY)

A people without knowledge of its history is like a tree without roots.

1. **In the past, I thought Africa was . . .**

   Now I know that it is . . .

2. **In the past, I thought African people were . . .**

   Now I know that they are . . .

SESSION 7: UJAMAA (COOPERATIVE ECONOMICS)

Let not what you cannot do tear from your hands what you can do.

1. **List two products or services that are available in your community.**

2. **Do you use these products or services? Why or why not?**

3. **List one thing that you could do to help make your community economically stronger.**

SESSION 8: KUUMBA (CREATIVITY)

With your hands you make your success,
with your hands you destroy your success.

1. **What is one ability, skill, or talent that you feel good about?**

2. **Who can you share this ability, skill, or talent with?**

3. **What is one thing you could do to improve your ability or talent?**

SESSION 9: NIA (PURPOSE)

Knowledge is like a garden: if it is not cultivated, it cannot be harvested.

Lack of knowledge is darker than night.

1. **What are two ways to cultivate your knowledge in school?**

2. **What are two ways to cultivate your knowledge in the community?**

SESSION 10: IMANI (FAITH)

Give a man a fish and he will eat for a day;
teach a man to fish and he will eat for a lifetime.

Be unable to handle an ax, but don't be unable to handle instruction.

1. **What does FAITH mean to you?**

2. **Do you think these proverbs are true? Why or why not?**

SESSION 11: KUJICHAGULIA (SELF-DETERMINATION)

The beak of the bird is what tells us the things it eats.

1. **What do you think are some of the major problems facing African American males?**

2. **When you hear the negtive statistics about African American males, how do you feel?**

3. **How can you change these statistics?**

SESSION 12: HESHEMA (RESPECT)

It is better to be loved than to be feared.

1. **Why is respect important?**

2. **How can you show respect to yourself?**

3. **What are important ways to show respect to others?**

4. **How can you handle a situation when you think someone is not showing you respect?**

SESSION 13: UJIMA (COLLECTIVE WORK AND RESPONSIBILITY)

Lead by example.

1. **What are two qualities of a positive leader?**

2. **What does positive peer pressure feel like?**

3. **Name two things you can do to be a positive leader.**

STAYING IN FOCUS ASSIGNMENTS

Session 2: *Nia* (Purpose) Staying in Focus Assignment:

Between now and the next session, practice two of your *jamaa* rules with your family or at school.

Session 3: *Kujichagulia* (Self-Determination) Staying in Focus Assignment:

Select one thing your *jamaa* will do before the next session to practice good health and fitness. How will you help one another in achieving this?

Session 4: *Umoja* (Unity) Staying in Focus Assignment:

Identify two African American men who have made an important contribution to their community. Learn something new about these men to share with your *jamaa*.

Session 5: *Umoja* (Unity) Staying in Focus Assignment:

Choose two countries in Africa. Learn something new about these countries to share with your *jamaa* at the next session.

Session 6: *Umoja* (Unity) Staying in Focus Assignment:

Share one new thing you've learned about Africa with someone not in the *Brothers of Ujima* program.

Session 7: *Ujamaa* (Cooperative Economics) Staying in Focus Assignment:

Do one positive thing for someone before the next session.

Session 8: *Kuumba* (Creativity) Staying in Focus Assignment:

Identify one way in which you express your creativity. Practice this before the next session.

Session 9: *Nia* (Purpose) Staying in Focus Assignment:

Write down one educational goal. Locate and identify one resource that can help support you in achieving that educational goal.

Session 10: *Imani* (Faith) Staying in Focus Assignment:

Ask two people (adults or peers) who know you, whom you trust, and who support you, to tell you two abilities or talents that they believe you have.

Session 11: *Kujichagulia* (Self Determination) Staying in Focus Assignment:

Share one new thing you've learned with someone not in the *Brothers of Ujima* program.

Session 12: *Heshema* (Respect) Staying in Focus Assignment:

Identify one difficult situation you have faced. Consider how well you handled the situation. Is there anything you could have done to handle the situation better?

Session 13: *Ujima* (Collective Work and Responsibility) Staying in Focus Assignment:

Identify two African American leaders you admire. Describe what it is that you admire about them.

APPENDIX B

Program Posters

BROTHERS OF UJIMA CREED

We will learn about and trust our talents and abilities.

We accept responsibility for what we do, who we are, and what we can become.

We will work to help each other by acknowledging and supporting the talents and gifts within our brothers, within ourselves, and within our community.

We will not act negatively toward or belittle our brothers, our sisters or our community.

We will show respect to our brothers, to ourselves, and to our community.

NGUZO NANE

EIGHT PRINCIPLES FOR AFRICAN AMERICAN LIVING

1. Umoja: Unity
2. Kujichagulia: Self-Determination
3. Ujima: Collective Work and Responsibility
4. Ujamaa: Cooperative Economics
5. Nia: Purpose
6. Kuumba: Creativity
7. Imani: Faith
8. Heshema: Respect

NGUZO/PRINCIPLE

UMOJA (UNITY)

NGUZO/PRINCIPLE

KUJICHAGULIA (SELF-DETERMINATION)

NGUZO/PRINCIPLE

UJIMA (TEAMWORK)

NGUZO/PRINCIPLE

UJAMAA
(COOPERATIVE ECONOMICS)

NGUZO/PRINCIPLE

NIA (PURPOSE)

NGUZO/PRINCIPLE

KUUMBA (CREATIVITY)

NGUZO/PRINCIPLE

IMANI (FAITH)

NGUZO/PRINCIPLE

HESHEMA (RESPECT)

Glossary

Durara umoja (*doo-RAH-rah oo-MOH-jah*)
Unity circle, symbolizing togetherness and support of one another

Heshema (*he-SHEM-mah*)
Respect (program principle)

Imani (*ee-MAH-nee*)
Faith (program principle)

Jamaa (*JAH-mah*)
Family or group

Kikombe cha Umoja (*kee-KOHM-bay cha oo-MOH-jah*)
The Unity Cup used in the Kwanzaa celebration

Kinara (*kee-NAH-rah*)
Candle holder used in the Kwanzaa celebration

Kujichagulia (*koo-jee-chah-goo-LEE-ah*)
Self-determination (program principle)

Kuumba (*koo-OOM-bah*)
Creativity (program principle)

Mazao (*mah-ZAH-oh*)
Fruits and vegetables (crops) used in the Kwanzaa celebration

Mishumaa Saba (*mee-shoo-MAH SAH-bah*)
Seven candles representing the seven principles (*Nguzo Saba*) in the Kwanzaa celebration

Mkeka (*m-KAY-kah*)
Mat used in the Kwanzaa celebration

Muhindi (*moo-HEEN-dee*)
Corn used in the Kwanzaa celebration

Mzee (*m-ZAY*)
Respected elder

Nguzo Nane (*n-GOO-zoh NAH-nay*)
Eight (*Nane*) Principles (*Nguzo*) of African American living on which the *Brothers of Ujima* program is based

Nguzo Saba (*n-GOO-zoh SAH-bah*)
Seven (*Saba*) Principles (*Nguzo*) of Kwanzaa

Nia (*NEE-ah*)
Purpose (a program principle)

Tambiko (*tahm-BEE-koh*)
Libations, or the pouring of water into the earth in memory of ancestors

Ujamaa (*oo-JAH-mah*)
Cooperative economics (program principle)

Ujima (*oo-JEE-mah*)
Collective work and responsibility (program principle)

Umoja (*oo-MOH-jah*)
Unity (program principle)

Zawadi (*zah-WAH-dee*)
Gifts given as part of the Kwanzaa celebration

Suggested Readings and Resources

AFRICAN AMERICAN MALES AND YOUTH

Boyd-Franklin, Nancy, Franklin, A.J., and Toussant, Pamela A. *Boys Into Men: Raising Our African-American Teenage Sons.* New York: Plume Books, 2003.

This book addresses the unique challenges of raising African American boys and provides advice to parents, teachers, counselors, and community members by drawing on African American family values and cultural and spiritual strengths.

Stevenson, Howard C. (editor). *Playing with Anger: Teaching Coping Skills to African American Boys through Athletics and Culture.* Westport, CT: Greenwood Publishing Group, 2003.

This book provides interventions designed for African American boys, especially those with a history of aggression. These interventions teach boys to manage their anger and use good coping skills through athletics such as basketball and martial arts.

Fashola, Olatokunbo S. (editor). *Educating African American Males: Voices from the Field.* Thousand Oaks, CA: Corwin Press, 2005.

This book provides several resources and offers diverse perspectives to understand and improve academic achievement of African American males.

Hale, Janice E. *Learning while Black: Creating Educational Excellence for African American Children.* Baltimore: Johns Hopkins University Press, 2001.

This book explores why Black children are not educated as well as White children. The author argues that educators must look beyond the cliches of urban poverty and teacher training to explain the failures of public education with regard to black students.

Kincheloe, Joe L., and hayes, kecia (editors). *Teaching City Kids: Understanding and Appreciating Them.* New York: Peter Lang Publishing, Inc. 2007.

This book provides a multilevel integrative approach to educating urban youth at the elementary, middle school, and high school levels. The approach takes into account historical, community, and cultural influences on the lives of these youth and incorporates these perspectives into their educational initiatives, including college preparatory programs.

Hrabowski, Freeman A., III, Maton, Kenneth I., and Greif, Geoffrey L. *Beating the Odds: Raising Academically Successful African American Males.* New York: Oxford University Press, 1998.

This book examines the role of parental factors, especially relationships, upon high academic achievement among African American males.

Hall, Horace B. *Mentoring Young Men of Color: Meeting the Needs of African American and Latino Students.* Lanham, MD: Rowman and Littlefield Education, 2006.

This book looks at a successful mentoring program for African American and Latino youth. The book provides valuable information on strategies to use to motivate these youth to improve academic performance and other positive behaviors and to reduce and prevent negative behaviors.

Franklin, Anderson J. *From Brotherhood to Manhood: How Black Men Rescue Their Relationships and Dreams from the Invisibility Syndrome.* New York: Wiley, 2004.

Dr. Franklin provides clinical insight into the challenges of being Black and male in America. The author's clinical work with Black men is the basis for his advice on how to confront these challenges and make a smooth transition into manhood.

Harris, Yvette R., and James A. Graham. *The African American Child: Development and Challenges.* New York: Springer Publishing Company, 2007.

This book makes the case that children's cultural differences need to be recognized for any accurate understanding of their development. It introduces readers to issues that have an impact on the lives of African American children but typically have been ignored or inadequately discussed in mainstream child development textbooks.

Toussaint, Pamela. *Great Books for African-American Children.* New York: Plume, 1999.

This annotated bibliography lists many books by and about African Americans that portray African Americans in a positive way.

Hopson, Darlene Powell, Hopson, Derek S., and Clavin, Thomas. *Juba this and Juba that: 100 African-American games for children.* New York: Simon and Schuster, 1996.

This book provides instructions for playing 100 board games, outdoor games, and other types of games and activities that celebrate the cultural heritage of Africa and African Americans. Instructions, age range, and equipment needed are included.

AFRICAN AMERICANS AND AFRICA

Appiah, K.A. *In My Father's House: Africa in the Philosophy of Culture.* New York: Oxford University Press, 1992.

Dodson, H. *Jubilee: The Emergence of African American Culture.* Washington, DC: National Geographic Books, 2003.

About the Authors

Faye Z. Belgrave is professor of psychology and the founding director of the Center for Cultural Experiences in Prevention at Virginia Commonwealth University. Her programmatic and research interests are in the areas of drug and HIV prevention among African Americans and other ethnic minorities. Much of her work has been conducted collaboratively with community organizations and is aimed at promoting positive youth development by increasing positive cultural values and preventing risky behaviors. This has included work on gender and culturally specific interventions. Dr. Belgrave has published extensively in the area of African American psychology and is an invited speaker on this topic. She has been recognized with many awards for her research, teaching, and service, including awards from the Association of Black Psychologists, the American Psychological Association, and the Substance Abuse and Mental Health Administration. Dr. Belgrave received her Ph.D. from the University of Maryland and her BS from North Carolina Agricultural and Technical State University.

Kevin W. Allison currently serves as the associate dean for community activities in the College of Humanities and Sciences at Virginia Commonwealth University and is a professor in psychology and in the L. Douglas Wilder School of Government and Public Affairs. He received his Ph.D. in clinical community psychology from DePaul University, and his undergraduate degree from the University of Notre Dame. Dr. Allison has been involved in the development and evaluation of school and community interventions supporting healthy developmental trajectories for urban youth. He serves as the associate director of the VCU Clark-Hill Institute for Positive Youth Development, one of the Centers for Disease Control National Academic Centers of Excellence on Youth Violence Prevention. Dr. Allison is also the co-author with Dr. Faye Belgrave of *African American Psychology: From Africa to America.*

Jerome Wilson is a man with a passion for youth. Much of his professional work has involved helping to support positive youth development. He was the project coordinator for the *Brothers of Ujima* program while employed at Virginia Commonwealth University. Jerome earned his undergraduate degree from Elizabeth City State University and his master's degree from Virginia Union School of Theology. Jerome's goal in life is to see that all children grow to become the future success stories they were born to be.

Raymond Tademy received his doctorate from Virginia Commonwealth University. He is currently the program evaluator for the Raise 5 Project, an HIV/AIDS and substance abuse prevention program conducted by the Center for Cultural Experiences in Prevention at Virginia Commonwealth University. Dr. Tademy has conducted programs and research on African American male health, substance abuse, and HIV prevention. He also mentors African American males who have been recently released from prison to assist in their reentry process. Dr. Tademy is also a military veteran, having served 25 years in the United States Marine Corps.